to Spreading Her Wings)

"Trish encourages women to challenge unfulfilling expectations, unhealthy emotional responses, incongruent spiritual practices and other behaviors that are blocking them from experiencing self-actualized lives. She provokes the reader to dig deep in exploring how these issues cause pain, restrict growth and result in patterns inconsistent with her desires. Each chapter is punctuated with specific strategies to assist women in moving their lives out of unfulfilling cycles into peace, freedom and true purpose. Trish courageously shares her own struggles and disappointments which allows the reader to realize that she is not alone in the journey of growth and healing. This is a must-read for any women, especially Black women, looking to break free and take flight in the next chapter of her life!"

- Regina S. Brown, PsyD, Licensed Psychologist

"Grab your journals, pens and smudge sticks! This self-help memoir is a refreshing guide on how you can begin the journey of making meaningful changes in your life to move outside of your chrysalis. Trish draws you in with her journey of healing and self-development. Through very personal narratives, she leads by example and shows us all that we can each start in one form, only to evolve into a better version of ourselves. We all just need a little courage to start the process. If you are looking to evolve, then this book is for you!"

- Natasha Brewley (Chef Beee), MBA, PhD, HHC
  Owner of Essentially Chef Beee
  and Nyansapo Wellness Institute, Inc.

"Trish Ahjel Roberts draws on her lived experiences with generosity and skill, presenting a '12-drop' approach to creating a more self-actualized (and joyful) life. *Thinking Outside the Chrysalis* is 'A Black Woman's Guide to Spreading Her Wings,' but Trish's perspective offers something for all women everywhere looking to live a more authentic life."

- Julie Hartley, MFA
  Director, Centauri Arts Writing School, Ontario, CN

"There is so much going on in the world that it's easy to lose your way, especially as a young woman of color in America right now. This book really helped me dive into my deeper self to help me start living my life comfortably as my truest self."

- Mona Swain, Theater Actress and TikTok Influencer

"Trish's book is a 12-step guide to an authentic and joyful life, not just for black women, but for anyone. This slim volume contains a lifetime of work. So many self-help tomes neglect her first piece of advice: Heal the Past First. They encourage action towards the future without first addressing the past, which often anchors us in place. She weaves in stories from her own life, as well as wisdom from the Buddhist tradition that she and I share. For example, the chapters on anger and patience are teachings of Buddha on how to live a life of peace and love. Trish offers numerous ways to stay engaged and positive as we break out of our chrysalis, including books, music and movies for inspiration and motivation. She tells her unique story as a single black mother at odds with a culture that dictates conformity instead of individuality. I recommend this book to anyone looking to develop their own personal identity and path."

- Paul B. Chen, Publisher, *Natural Awakenings - Atlanta*

"This is a perfect book for anyone beginning their journey of self-discovery or even in the thick of working to figure things out. Trish shows us how beautiful this process of growth and transformation can be when we listen to our inner calling and step bravely into who we're meant to be."

- Jaimee Ratliff
  Owner, Yoga with Jaimee, LLC

"I am so inspired by Trish. She completely shares herself and her wisdom in this book. I felt like I had a conversation with a therapist without actually having to divulge all my 'stuff,' even while she helped me comb through it. Real talk! Following each chapter, she gives a guide to help you process deep feelings that may have arisen. (Let's pollinate!) Finally, she makes it all light with music and movie selections that reflect each chapter's theme. Totally feeling this book!"

- Sonia Kidd, Coaching Client and Business Owner

"Trish and I are friends so my perspective might be a little biased, but also a bit deeper. I've had the opportunity to work with her as a coaching client and on my own through many of the resources in each chapter of her beautiful book. She provides such a lovely framework to search deeper into your heart's desires and passions, while giving you the courage to flutter and realize your authentic self. This book has really inspired me and gently nudged me to think about the possibilities in my life in a different way. Trish provides the roadmap to start a beautiful journey, no matter where you are in your life."

- Tamara Guillou, Coaching Client
  and Corporate Executive

"So many of us are moving through our daily lives without stopping to consider if we could be doing more, giving more, being more. This book poses the questions many of us don't think to ask. Trish offers a fresh perspective that challenges us to open to new possibilities and become our best selves. Her words are so liberating and inspirational, she lit a fire inside of me! I can't wait to see where her 12-drop process takes me."

- Lisa Martin Suber, Children's Book Author
  and Atlanta Public School Teacher

"If you're looking for a sign, consider this it. My mom's self-help memoir will change your outlook on life if you give it the power to do so. Her words embolden women of color to take the reins of their own lives. She inspires readers to never settle for mediocrity, embrace change, and dream BIG! Enough of sitting around and hoping for good to come. This is the key to all of your locked doors."

- Kayla George, Student, University of Georgia

"*Thinking Outside the Chrysalis* is a must-read for any woman who is dissatisfied with her life, stuck in old habits or simply searching for a greater connection with self. Trish addresses difficult topics that most of us just hope will fade into the background and never return again, not realizing that if we don't come to terms with our past, we cannot create a fully abundant future. Trish guides us down this path with humor, humility, and compassion. I personally feel a greater connection with self, women of color, and the world at large as a result of this book."

- Cindy Parker, Administrative Director,
  Kadampa Meditation Center, Atlanta GA

Thinking Outside the Chrysalis

(A Black Woman's Guide to Spreading Her Wings)

A SELF-HELP MEMOIR

by

Trish Ahjel Roberts

The author and the publisher have made every effort to ensure that the information in this book is correct. The events, locales, and conversations are based on the author's memories of them. Some names and identifying details have been changed or omitted to protect the privacy of individuals.

The author is not responsible for websites (or their content) that are not owned by the author. Every effort has been made to correctly reference music, film, and other resources. Any inadvertent errors will gladly be rectified.

© Copyright 2020 Thinking Outside the Chrysalis: A Black Woman's Guide to Spreading Her Wings by Trish Ahjel Roberts

All rights reserved. Except as permitted under the U.S. Copyright Act of 1976, no part of this publication may be reproduced, distributed, or transmitted in any form or by any means, or stored in a database or retrieval system, without the prior written permission of the copyright owner.

For permissions or corrections:
Email hello@trishahjelroberts.com

First Edition: July 2020

Printed in the United States of America

Cover design by:
Oliviaprodesign

Photo credit:
Trish Ahjel Roberts

ISBN: 9798653338618

Also by

Trish Ahjel Roberts

12 Steps to Mind-Blowing Happiness:
A Journal of Insights, Quotes & Questions
to Juice Up Your Journey

Mind-Blowing Happiness™ Guide to Self-Care
(e-book)

Chocolate Soufflé
(a novel)

My mother always said
I could do anything I set my mind to.
For a long time, I didn't believe it was true.
Now I know it is.
This book is for Mommie.
I hope you can read it from wherever you are.

My father always said
I have to know who I am.
For a long time, I didn't know what he meant.
Now I do.
This book is for Daddy.
I hope you're proud of me.

My grandmother always said
the young may die, but the old must die.
For a long time, I didn't understand what she meant.
Now I do.
This book is for Mamma.
I hope you are getting the rest you deserve.

For all my ancestors known and unknown.

Thank you.

Acknowledgements

I owe the biggest, loudest thank you to my long-time BFF, Tamara Guillou, for being my pro-bono business consultant, first-draft editor, market tester, midnight book reader, giggle buddy and all-around amazing person. She's been the first to read every blog, newsletter and chapter, always available with invaluable feedback and encouragement on my creative journey.

Thank you to everyone who's taken the time to read my book in advance and offer a heartfelt testimonial: Natasha Brewley, Regina Brown, Paul Chen, Kayla George, Tamara Guillou, Julie Hartley, Sonia Kidd, Cindy Parker, Jaimee Ratliff, Lisa Suber, Mona Swain. Your feedback fills my heart with joy and confirms I'm on the right path. I am forever grateful.

Thank you to my Black Vegan Life™ advisory board members for taking time out of your busy schedules to listen to my dreams and offer guidance: Ebony Dixon, Jackie Fairley, Tamara Guillou, Cat Johnson, Melissa Jones, Sonia Kidd, Tiffani Tucker, Eric Williams. You believed in me when I had nothing to offer but a desire to explore my own potential. Your support has been invaluable.

Thank you to my daughter, Kayla, for your ongoing love and hilarious commentary. Thank you to my sister Chrissy for always encouraging my writing. Thank you to my nephew Carlee for holding down the Brooklyn crew. Thank you to my sister, Nisey, for giving me a book that changed my life so many years ago and for supporting my journey as a writer. Thank you to my high school bestie, Melanie, for loving me and my family for nearly forty years. And, thank you to my canine assistant, Cooper, for being a wonderful lap warmer and snuggle buddy. I love you all.

Contents

Preparing the Caterpillar / 15

Drop 1: Heal the Past First / 23

Drop 2: Get a (Spiritual) Life / 33

Drop 3: It Takes a Village (to Support an Adult) / 39

Drop 4: Get REAL with Someone / 47

Drop 5: Anger is a Lie / 57

Drop 6: Give it Away for Free / 69

Drop 7: No More Bag Lady / 77

Drop 8: Lay Your Weapons Down / 91

Drop 9: Patience is the Truth / 101

Drop 10: Don't Eat the Dead / 111

Drop 11: Work Equals Play / 129

Drop 12: Float Like a Butterfly / 141

Questions for Your Kaleidoscope / 149

Notes / 155

Nectar Bowl (A Place to Collect Your Thoughts) / 159

Preparing the Caterpillar
(Please Read This First!)

The Greek origin of the word "chrysalis," or butterfly cocoon, means "gold." The shell that encloses us is often a beautiful façade that keeps us trapped in complacency – the family, home, friends, career, cars and other possessions at first glance seem satisfying. However, despite per capita wealth, most Americans are not any happier than people living in less affluent parts of the world.[1] We enjoy entertainment and special occasions, but we struggle to get ahead, feel secure and understand our life's purpose or why we must endure painful events. Sadness, anxiety, restlessness and depression are epidemic.[2] The coronavirus pandemic poured gasoline on what was already ablaze. We are a nation of daily stress and distractions.

Sometimes the shell isn't so golden – we may not have a support network or appropriate resources, and physical or psychological abuse may heighten the sense of limitations on what we believe to be possible. My childhood was underscored by trauma which constructed a sturdy chrysalis. After years of conspicuous camouflage, I found myself on a quest to emerge in full expression of my authentic self. I believe self-actualization is the ultimate goal for humans, and it's taken me a long time to identify my passions and have the courage to live them. This butterfly has spread her wings.

Oxford defines self-actualization as "the realization of fulfillment of one's talents and potentialities, especially considered as a drive or need present in everyone." According to Maslow's Need Hierarchy once the basic requirements for food, shelter, safety, community, and self-esteem are met, people intrinsically seek this highest realization.

I created this book to show you how to recognize your own passions and develop the audacity to break away from the routine and live your most deeply authentic and wildly joyful life. Butterflies feed on drops of nectar. With a simple 12-drop approach, you will receive the nourishment you need to soar through life with the ease of a butterfly.

**Anyone can benefit from this book,
but it is my unapologetic love letter to Black women.**

Our thinking is what often limits us. If we believe there is nothing outside of our cocoon, we can never have a breakthrough. We first must have a "think-through," believing in the effortless abundance waiting for us beyond our mental constraints. This book uses my real-life experiences, along with Buddhist and yogic philosophies to help shine light on the freedom on the other side of the chrysalis.

**This book is for people who want more.
More joy. More love. More connection.
More freedom. More happiness.**

Just because my 12-drop approach is simple doesn't mean it's easy. This isn't a get-rich-quick scheme. I can't guarantee you will have a breakthrough overnight. Placing this book on your nightstand while you sleep will not change your life. Posting it on social media won't either (although sharing is caring, and I would love for you to spread the word). Even reading through this book completely won't have a big impact without a commitment to take action.

I absolutely guarantee that working through the reflection questions, repeating the affirmations, setting goals and performing action steps (what I call "pollinating") and participating in the guided meditations at the end of each chapter, or "drop" will manifest positive change in your life.

If you go a step further, and work with an accountability partner and explore recommended resources, change will come faster and will be even more profound. (If you self-identify as a Black woman, you can look for an accountability partner in the Black Girl Butterflyz Facebook community.)

**This book is not for everyone.
It's for people who are willing to put in some effort to create their most joyful and fulfilling life.**

I work regularly with successful Black women as a life coach specializing in self-actualization. There are eight main areas of life that I address with my clients:

- Mental health and personal development
- Relationships
- Physical health
- Spiritual life
- Occupation
- Fun and recreation
- Money
- Physical environment (home/work)

The ability to "think outside the chrysalis" and achieve self-actualization flows into all areas. Afterall, you can't fulfill your talents at the highest levels if you haven't nurtured healthy relationships, can't afford to pay your rent, or are stuck in a battle with physical or mental illness.

You have probably heard of Napoleon Hill's *Think and Grow Rich*. I read it in my early twenties when I lived in East

Flatbush, Brooklyn and longed for the American Dream. I wanted wealth and love, exactly in that order. I used to have subscriptions to *Black Enterprise* and *The Wall Street Journal* along with the requisite *Essence, Ebony* and later, *O Magazine*. This Black girl capitalist drank all the Kool-Aid. While I still believe in free enterprise, over the years I've transformed into the person I always wanted to be but was too scared to become: author, entrepreneur, activist, yogi, vegan, Buddhist, meditation instructor and environmentalist. Money is nice and necessary, but my life is no longer built around its pursuit. Even love and marriage don't have the place they once did. As a hetero woman, I think men are sexy and wonderful, but they are not a determinant of my happiness. I have found the summit of my personal joy through a life well-lived, surrounded by community, love and peace. My joy isn't based on things or people I can't control. My mornings are rich with gratitude. I spend my days engaged in activities I would do for free while getting paid for it. I sleep like a baby at night knowing I'm contributing as much good as I can to this world. I know I am on the right side of history, and I am part of the solution to the world's many problems.

The breakthrough happened when I dared to think outside the norm of what I had been taught were my life options, or what should be my goals.
I call this "Thinking Outside the Chrysalis."

If you're anything like me, you like to know what to expect before you start a new venture. Here's the deal. This is a workbook. Each chapter is a "drop." You may want to go through a drop per week, a drop per month, a drop per quarter or a drop per year. It's up to you. After each drop there's a worksheet to help you process the information that was given as it relates to your own life.

You might want to read through the entire book for an overview and then go back to work through the chapters. I recommend you keep a companion notebook to write your answers to the reflection questions, document your action steps or "pollination" and journal your feelings at the end of each chapter. I love old school composition books and pretty journals. If you're more new school, you might want to try one of the many digital journaling apps available.

**Set aside some time,
make sure your journal is safe and private,
and commit to enjoying the process.
This is unapologetic, radical self-love time for YOU.**

At the end of each drop you will find uplifting songs, or "grooves for fluttering" and helpful movies and documentaries, or "think-through films." Art provides a profound way to absorb and reinforce information, plus it's beautiful. No matter who we are, we can all use more beauty in our lives. All resources can be accessed through TrishAhjelRoberts.com/resources. Finally, each drop has additional resources to support your journey. I only included information that I've used myself or has come highly recommended from someone in my close personal network. There are a few pages in the back of this book for your notes, so you never find yourself stuck with an *aha!* moment and no place to write. Unearthing can be painful at times - use this mantra as a reminder. You can record in your smartphone and listen on a loop, or you can find all affirmations in this book recorded for you at TrishAhjelRoberts.com/resources.

***I enjoy getting to know and heal my true self.
I won't give up.
What's on the other side is more beautiful
than I can imagine.
I'm worth every minute of this.***

Look out for bold and italicized points throughout the book. These are items you may want to revisit. The "drops" are given to you in an order for a reason, however, feel free to work through them in any order that makes sense to you. This is your journey.

When I teach yoga, I always tell my clients it should feel *good*. It doesn't mean you don't feel what we refer to as an "edge." It may be intensely challenging, awkward or somewhat uncomfortable, but there is still a good feeling throughout – a feeling of expansion and opening that is very sweet. If it's too painful, we stop. Our body lets us know today's not the day. We can try again later. This book should feel the same – like a deep stretch, a gentle backbend, an extension way up toward the sun and then down deep to the earth – like a quiet exploration of your heart. *It may be achy, but if it's deeply painful, today's not the day. It's okay to take a break and come back.*

Expansion takes time in the body and in the mind. Through this openness I have found Freedom, Alignment and Effortless Abundance for myself. These are my words for self-actualization. From the depth of my heart, I wish the same for you.

Take a moment and write down your intention for reading this book. Don't overthink it, just quickly jot down what rises in your heart:

_____
_____
_____
_____

As you go through each drop, there are a few lines underneath the heading. This is an excellent place to jot down your intention for that particular chapter or use as a reminder to write in your journal. *What made you pick up this book or chapter today? What do you hope to learn? What do you hope to release?*

Finally, you might want to use this book in a group environment – perhaps with your book club, church group or moms' club. You can discuss the worksheet at the end of each drop or discuss the entire book in a single conversation. I've included discussion questions at the end for that purpose.

Now that you know what to expect and how this little book can take your life to new levels of joy and fulfillment, let's get started!

First Drop: Heal the Past First

"If you're silent about your pain,
they'll kill you and say you enjoyed it."
- Zora Neale Hurston

_____
_____
_____
_____

This is the first drop for a reason. The past is the beginning. Our childhood is the foundation for our adult lives. I enjoyed a middle-class childhood in a loving, two-parent home in Brooklyn, NY. I attended a private junior high school and a prestigious public high school in Manhattan. I had the opportunity to go to college and earn a master's degree while working for a Fortune 100 company. Despite my good fortune and accomplishments, I never felt good *enough*. In my twenties, I wondered why smart and interesting men wanted to date me. *What did they see in me?* I remember telling my sister through drunken tears that I always felt like a broken doll. That was twenty years ago. I was in my early thirties then and had finally found words to embody my emotions. The brokenness was so deep, it took years before I could even verbalize it.

I am educated. My mother had a sprawling collection of books and read to me every night. My first memory is reading the *New York Times* with my mom when I was four years old and picking out words that I knew. I was reading at a twelfth-grade level when I was in fifth grade. My IQ was above 130 when I was in middle school. I come from a supportive family. I had access to a reasonable amount of resources. I cannot even imagine what my life would have been like if I didn't have the love of my family, even when they didn't have the bandwidth to process the trauma I was attempting to manage with my young mind. My parents nearly divorced because they were in the orbit of my suffering.

I believe every negative experience has the potential to grow you or destroy you. I've learned it is impossible to live the life of your dreams with an unhealed heart.

Child sexual abuse and domestic violence are epidemic in the U.S.[1,2] I've experienced both, and they aren't unrelated. I carried shame and trauma through my pre-teens and into my thirties. I remember reading Maya Angelou's *I Know Why the Caged Bird Sings*. I couldn't believe she let the world know she was raped as a child. It was my deepest shame, and I couldn't speak those words. I marveled at the fact that a human had so much courage. That is one of many books that probably saved my life, exemplifying the profound importance of literacy. Standing on the shoulders of Maya Angelou, I found the beginnings of a voice. I began to speak my truth in my circle of friends. My fourteen-year-old mind was angry for being held responsible for something that wasn't my fault. I wore black all the time, ran away from home, smoked Newports and numbed myself with alcohol. I discovered I wasn't alone. Friend after friend told me they had similar experiences. Not only girls, but boys too.

My friends and I used to hang out at my high school counselor's office cutting class and smoking cigarettes. Later, my parents took me a psychologist who told them I was probably hooked on cocaine. I wasn't and bawled uncontrollably. Those were my first encounters with counseling – one "fun," one terrible, both completely useless.

The next time I walked into a therapist's office was to see a marriage counselor. I was embarrassed to walk into the building with the big red letters, "MENTAL HEALTH." *Couldn't they be more discreet?* I didn't want anyone to think there was something wrong with me. When I met with the therapist, I mentioned my childhood trauma, thinking it might be affecting my relationship. The therapist quipped, "That was in the past. I want to talk about what's happening now," and completely dismissed my proposal. She encouraged me to get pregnant even though I didn't have confidence in my relationship. One day my husband and I showed up for an appointment only to find out she had died. We were stunned, and the staff was apologetic. The new therapist rolled her eyes in frustration because she didn't understand why I hadn't already left my husband. In retrospect, I don't think either one was helpful, although it did affect my decision to get pregnant. I am grateful for my beautiful daughter, although my marriage quickly crumbled. I think if I had waited for the right man and the right time, I never would have become a mother.

My sister gave me *The Courage to Heal* books by Ellen Bass and Laura Davis when I was in my early thirties (after the drunken crying and right after the collapse of my marriage). It was such an unexpected blessing. Finally, I had a resource to work through my trauma. I recommend those books all the time and everywhere. It was profoundly helpful to me.

The next time I saw a therapist was when I was being pushed out of a job that I loved in a massive racial cleansing. Every Black person in my position was fired or pressured to resign over the course of about two years, and it was my turn. I was stressed out. My eyes were twitching. I couldn't think clearly. I had done everything I thought was possible to perform at the levels required of me, but ultimately, it wasn't realistic. Our new objectives were designed to be unattainable, and the "performance improvement plan" that was put in place was a thinly veiled exit ramp. I took my crumpled-up spirit to a soft-spoken, laid-back white man who asked about my sleep and told me to look for another job. I took a mental health leave to catch my breath before the guillotine landed on my neck. I had worked at the company for nearly eight years as a sales executive. It was my job to promote the firm. They often show up on those lists of best places to work, and they tossed me and about thirty of my Black colleagues out like garbage.

After being pushed out of my six-figure job and working for a year making half my salary at a local college, I decided to purchase a small fitness franchise. I thought it would allow me to work with integrity, stay close to my young daughter, get my income back on track and chart my own path. I learned plenty from the experience and had the opportunity to advocate for survivors during that time by hosting a film screening and speaking at a local community center. However, I was dead wrong about getting my income back on track. The business failed, and I had to sell the house I loved. I felt like I couldn't catch a break.

I didn't see another therapist until I was living in Atlanta in 2008. I decided to make the move because I could no longer afford to live in Brooklyn. My sister had moved down with her family a few years before and liked it, so it seemed like a good plan. I imagined southern hospitality and good weather. I got the weather I wanted, but the culture was far more overtly racist and cliquish than New York – a far cry from hospitable.

Against my better judgment, I decided to pursue a career in the blatantly racist and sexist finance industry. I hadn't yet learned to consider my race in every life choice that I made. I started working in the supposed "Black mecca" at a major brokerage firm with a staff of fifty white financial advisors and one Black guy who came every Tuesday to shine shoes. *What planet had I settled on?* To be fair, there was one Black financial advisor, who disappeared while I was still in training. There was also a Black guy who worked in a support role. So out of a staff of about seventy-five, there was one Black guy and me. I was there for a year and was devastated when I was forced to move on. The industry is known for what they call "churn and burn," hiring many financial advisors and seeing who can bring in the millions of dollars of investor assets required to survive.

It's virtually impossible if the firm doesn't provide support through mentoring or teaming opportunities. A number of large firms have reached class action settlements because of the structural racism and sexism which was uncovered. This particular firm was paying out settlement money to the female financial advisors when I first started working there. Since then, I've been part of two class action lawsuits at other large financial institutions. My story isn't unique. It plays out again and again across corporate America in much the same way police brutality does – like an old school broken record.

I was beyond stressed out and continued to advocate for my own mental health. The first therapist I met with in Atlanta told me to wear eye shadow to fight racism and sexism. She said it would increase my confidence – basically make me the baddest bitch in the room. (Insert eye roll.) I upgraded my makeup palette to include not only my standard mascara, but eye shadow. Crazy, but it was the recommendation from a qualified therapist, so I did it.

I found a competent therapist to help unpack my emotional baggage shortly after; she apologized for the eyeshadow lady and the marriage counselor who was unwilling to talk about my childhood. I saw six counselors before landing upon someone who was not only capable but willing to help me. I was determined to grow personally and advocate for myself. I imagine today there is more therapy available for sexually assaulted kids. We've come a long way since the '70s and '80s.

Many of us experience trauma or negative events that stunt our emotional or spiritual development. By reading self-help books like *The Courage to Heal*, watching films that tackled the subject matter, working with a real-life therapist, opening up with friends and family and learning to stand in my truth, I've been able to heal.

I know we all have a wide range of experiences with trauma and healing. For Black women, racial trauma is par for the course even if it's our only negative experience. If the path toward healing resonates with you, consider your financial and family support situation. I know it's different for all of us. You may want to join a support group if you can't find helpful souls in your personal network, or if you simply want more anonymity. Therapy through art, nature or interaction with animals is also worth exploring, whether in a formal or informal way. I cannot say that these methods have been part of my healing from trauma, but I believe my love and enjoyment of painting and viewing art, hiking and visiting animal sanctuaries has lowered the levels of stress in my life and contributed to my overall wellness. The beautiful thing about living in the age of technology is that we have vast resources at our fingertips, and most folks have access to a smartphone if not a full computer.

The mind is fascinating in its ability to be self-protective. Our minds can rewire to protect us from the effects of physical or emotional trauma. That's why some people develop disassociations or blocked memories, and many times we don't even know why we do the things we do.[3] I know I spent years hiding, at least partially, behind my first husband's last name. Even though he was physically violent with me, using his name allowed me to disconnect from my past.

Getting good therapy helps us unpack our past hurts so we can fully experience our present with a new lightness.

Be prepared. Even when you find someone willing and able to help, or a meaningful resource to guide you, it's still not easy. It takes commitment and time. There will be pain as long-buried emotions rise to the surface. You may experience denial and anger. All of this is okay. Therapy can be with a person, an app or a book. It could be with a psychiatrist, psychologist or counselor. The main thing is that you find space to unpack your issues and lighten your load.

Our goal is to soar into our brilliance, and you can't do it with a brick on your back.

Be patient with yourself. Healing is an ongoing process, no matter what you're working on. You may heal a piece of what an abuser did, and a few years later heal from the isolation of your family. You may heal from how your parents disciplined or ridiculed you, and then discover another wounded piece of yourself. You may heal from an unhealthy relationship, and later discover the wounds run deeper than you thought. You may put a band-aid on a scratch and years later discover what was under the bandage is still infected. Don't approach the process of mental health as an open and shut case. Accept it as part of your ongoing journey of self-awareness and self-care. Most importantly, prioritize your healing.

Even if you had a happy childhood free from abuse or trauma, if you are a minority or a woman, you are oppressed in most societies. Therapy will likely be valuable.

> ***Healing is a gift to yourself***
> ***whether it's attained through formal or casual sources.***
> ***This is your body, your mind, your life.***
> ***Why not take the time to***
> ***explore and process your journey?***

I can guarantee if you ever find yourself in the final days of your life, you won't be saying, "I wish I watched more TV or drank more wine." My guess is you'll wonder about how you took up space in this world while you were in it. Did you love enough? Did you create enough? Did you evolve enough? Did you ever get to know yourself truly? Did you ever really know anyone else? Did you leave the world better for having lived in it? Did you love yourself enough to heal?

Affirmations for Healing:
- ❖ I am strong. I am a survivor. I am beyond resilient.
- ❖ I am good enough. I have done enough. I have enough.
- ❖ I can heal from my past. I grow from all my experiences.
    (Repeat at least 2x per day.)

Reflection Questions:
- ❖ What trauma or unhealed parts of me still cause pain when I remember them?
- ❖ Am I willing to advocate for my own healing?
- ❖ Am I willing to put in effort to heal from my past?

Write your response to the questions that resonate with you and continue journaling any feelings that arise from the questions or the chapter. Use these guidelines for all reflection questions in future drops.

Time to Get Still:
- ❖ Visit TrishAhjelRoberts.com/resources and access Meditation #1 for Healing.
    (Enjoy at least 2x per week, but daily is ideal.)

Let's Pollinate!

The work of the butterfly is to pollinate by absorbing drops of nectar and spreading growth. This is where we commit to actions that have the power to grow us deeply and transform us.

- ❖ Make a commitment to get therapy in some form to work through any parts of your past that require some healing. There are lots of options to choose from in the resource section to get you started.

- ❖ Set a SMART goal related to your healing: Specific, Measurable. Attainable, emotionally Relevant and Timebound. (For example, your goal might be to purchase a healing book and read it in the next two months, or to identify a counselor that you like and have a meeting within the next month.)
- ❖ Find an accountability partner to help you stick with your goal either through your circle of friends or in the Black Girl Butterflyz Facebook community. You don't have to share details of your goal, but you can share progress. (I am the group administrator, but I do not control group membership. You are responsible for relationships that you create in this group or any other.)

Grooves for Fluttering:
- ❖ Corinne Bailey Rae. "Butterfly." *Corrine Bailey Rae*, 2006.
- ❖ Maxwell. "Lifetime." *Now*, 2001.
- ❖ Destiny's Child. "Survivor." *This is the Remix*, 2002.
- ❖ Solange. "Cranes in the Sky." *A Seat at the Table*, 2016.

Think-Through Films:
- ❖ *Woman Thou Art Loosed*. Directed by Michael Schultz. Starring Kimberly Elise and Loretta Devine. Magnolia Pictures, 2004. Based on *Woman Though Art Loosed* by T.D. Jakes.
- ❖ *Enough*. Directed by Michael Apted. Starring Jennifer Lopez. Columbia Pictures, 2002.
- ❖ *Antwone Fisher*. Directed by Denzel Washington. Starring Derek Luke and Denzel Washington. Fox Searchlight Pictures, 2002.
- ❖ *Prince of Tides*. Directed by Barbara Streisand. Starring Barbara Streisand and Nick Nolte. Columbia Pictures, 1991.

Additional Resources:
- TrishAhjelRoberts.com/resources is your main portal for all resources.
- *The Courage to Heal* by Ellen Bass and Laura Davis
- *Get Over It!: Thought Therapy for Healing the Hard Stuff* by Iyanla Vanzant
- Psychologytoday.com
- TherapyforBlackgirls.com
- *The 1619 Project* (podcast)
- *The Body Keeps the Score* by Bessel Van Der Kolk, MD
- *Healing the Fragmented Selves of Trauma Survivors* by Janina Fisher
- Zocdoc.com
- Judi Ingram Adkins, mariettapsychotherapist.com
- Amazon, Audible, Google, YouTube and your local library

Second Drop: Get a (Spiritual) Life

"Believe in nothing, no matter where you read it, or who said it, no matter if I have said it, unless it agrees with your own reason and your own common sense."
- Buddha

_____
_____
_____
_____

As healing begins or matures from that first drop of nectar, it needs a foundation to rest upon. Spirituality is that base. Without a concept of a self beyond the physical, it's difficult to know who we're actually healing. We've all heard the term "inner child." I believe it goes deeper, to our inner spirit.

When I was in my thirties, I realized I am a spiritual being in a human body. I believe we all are. It doesn't mean I have to belong to a particular religion, but I know at some point I had to acknowledge there is a whole lot going on inside of me.

Although I was raised Catholic, I was an atheist from when I was a teenager until age thirty. I felt betrayed by the god of my youth, and I hadn't yet faced enough hardship as an adult to seek help beyond friends and family. It wasn't until I was older, and life got really *thick,* that I realized I needed more than just me. I remember thinking, *there must be more than this* – more meaning, more purpose, more help. From there, I began a spiritual journey that took me from Atheist, to Christian and now Buddhist. I don't believe any path has all the answers, but I believe each has some, whether it's Islam, Hinduism, Yoruba, Bahai, Wicca, Judaism, Voodoo or any of the many world religions. You may never become a card-carrying member of any of them, but in my experience taking the time to explore spirituality is its own prize.

There is a world that we see and a world that we can't see. Even the dust and the bacteria know that. They slip by us undetected. If you didn't believe it before, the pandemic of 2020 made us all disciples. The eyes are only a single sense. We perceive with our ears, nose, skin and mouth. We don't stop at five senses, though, because there isn't a single person on this earth without intuition – we perceive with our hearts, minds and souls. At times we may feel disconnected from this sixth sense, but it is always there, whether well-oiled or rusty. I know that exploring my inner self and honing my intuitive skills are activities I will never regret, not even on my death bed.

I have friends who identify strongly with the religion of their childhood and don't feel the need for a journey to anything else. Even if that's the case, I believe there is so much wisdom in the ancient experiences of others, who wouldn't want to explore in some way?

I belonged to a United Church of Christ (UCC) church when I lived in Brooklyn. We had a Black female pastor who spoke powerfully each week. I couldn't wait for her sermons. One week she asked, "Have you ever met someone who doesn't understand anything because they've never been through anything?" Such a poignant question. It made me realize how my own struggles had deepened my humanity and compassion. I'm embarrassed to admit it, but I wasn't immediately supportive when I learned she was gay. I didn't think I had any issues with homosexuality, but I didn't want a gay woman as my spiritual leader, so obviously I had a problem. I saw homosexuality as a sin like drinking or gambling. I don't know exactly when I shook off my own bias, but I'm glad I came to the realization that sexuality has nothing to do with spirituality. When I found Buddhism, it was a breath of fresh air. There was no story of creation, concept of sin or demands for tithing. I know a lot of my LGBTQ brothers and sisters have been traumatized by organized religion. I know some aspects of Christianity were deeply troubling for me. But, remember the old saying, don't throw the baby out with the bathwater?

> ***Even if a particular tradition didn't work for you, you are still a spiritual person.***

Part of the history of organized religion is to combine with government to control the populace. We still see this in many countries today where religious freedoms do not exist or are severely limited like China, North Korea and Iran.

In the U.S., while it wasn't technically the government, bible verses were used to keep enslaved people in mental bondage. For the few souls who were allowed to learn to read, they were first directed to Ephesians 6:5 where Paul says, "Slaves be obedient to your human masters with fear and trembling, in sincerity of heart, as to Christ." This is portrayed quite well in the 2016 film, *The Birth of a Nation*. The bible was also used by Puritans to hang women for witchcraft in seventeenth century Salem.[1] Remember spiritual books are still texts written by people. The Christian bible was written over the course of more than two decades, beginning forty years after the death of Christ.[2] Each gospel was selected and edited by those in power at a time when most of the population was illiterate. It doesn't mean that holy books don't have profound wisdom, but you would be remiss if you didn't use your own human intelligence and intuition when you read them. Any honorable deity would consent to that.

> ***Whatever you were taught as a child or have come to believe, you are missing out if you don't recognize your own Divine spiritual self.***

No matter your belief system, connection and support are critical. I have an atheist friend who belongs to a non-believer community. I'm not sure if it's considered a spiritual community, but it's certainly a support group. Flexibility is important too, because I'm confident that when the time of reckoning comes, we're all going to find out we weren't quite correct.

I changed churches a few times before stumbling into a Buddhist meditation center for a lunchtime session. I was hoping it would calm the inner rage over my racist boss and disappointing boyfriend. It did all of that and so much more and became my spiritual home. It nourishes me in all the most important ways.

No matter whether you believe in heaven, hell, reincarnation or eternal slumber, it's hard to deny that inside this shell of a body there is a fire – a light, a soul, a spirit, a mental continuum. It doesn't matter if you are atheist, agnostic, Seventh Day Adventist, Jehovah's Witness, Baptist, Muslim or anything else.

That little light of yours needs nurturing,
and it's not your physical body.
If you're not familiar with that inner spark,
it's time to start the expedition.
You won't find this precious jewel
if you're not even looking.

Finding a spiritual life that works for me has had a profound impact on my happiness. I've learned to lean in and fall back with the endless twists and turns of life. When I stumble, I'm able to regain my balance. When I fall, I find I'm able to get back up and carry on. My walk on this earth has been rife with winding trails and occasional potholes. I've learned to walk in gratitude and with resilience. I attribute that to my spiritual journey. It's foundational and has made all the difference in the world.

Affirmations for Spirit:
- There is a part of me that cannot be extinguished. My spirit is immortal.
- I nourish my spirit every day.
- I know there is a light inside of me. I will shine my goodness on others.

   (Repeat at least 2x per day.)

Reflection Questions:
- How would you describe your spiritual progression from childhood to adulthood?
- Are you fulfilled and nourished in your spiritual life?
- Is there anything you would like to change about your daily spiritual experience?

Time to Get Still:
- Visit TrishAhjelRoberts.com/resources and access Meditation #2 for Spirit.

  (Enjoy at least 2x per week, but daily is ideal.)

Let's Pollinate!
- Make a commitment to set aside time for spiritual growth. If you choose to explore other belief systems, think critically. You don't have to believe every idea that you encounter. Take what makes sense to you and leave the rest.
- Set a SMART goal: Specific, Measurable, Attainable, emotionally Relevant and Timebound
- Continue to work with your accountability partner.

Grooves for Fluttering:
- India Arie. "I Am Light." *Songversation*, 2013.
- Beyoncé. "Spirit." *The Lion King*, 2019.
- Joeboy. "Blessings." *Love & Light*, 2019.
- India Arie. "I See God in You." *Acoustic Soul*, 2001.

Think-Through Films:
- *The Story of God with Morgan Freeman.* Executive Producer, Morgan Freeman. National Geographic Channel, 2016.
- *The Shift.* Directed by Michael A. Goorjian. Starring Dr. Wayne W. Dyer. Produced by Marco Sanchez, 2009.
- *The Matrix.* Directed by Lana Wachowski. Starring Keanu Reeves and Laurence Fishburne. Warner Bros., 1999.
- *The Birth of a Nation.* Directed by Nate Parker. Starring Nate Parker and Gabrielle Union. Bron Studios, 2016.

Additional Resources:
- TrishAhjelRoberts.com/resources is your main portal for all resources.
- *How to Solve Our Human Problems* by Geshe Kelsang Gyatso
- *The Yamas and Niyamas* by Deborah Adele
- *The Road Less Traveled* by M. Scott Peck, M.D.
- *Teachings of the Master: The Collected Sayings of Jesus Christ,* compiled by Philip Law
- The New Living Translation Bible
- Kadampa.org
- UCC.org
- Amazon, Audible, Google, YouTube and your local library

Third Drop: It Takes a Village (to Support an Adult)

"If you want to go quickly, go alone.
If you want to go far, go together."
- African Proverb

_____
_____
_____
_____

Healing is a long process for many of us. Embarking on a spiritual journey also takes time. Those two activities alone are profound and powerful and will open doors to increasing wholeness and joy. I congratulate you if those are roads you choose to travel. No matter your path, you will need help from others.

Humans are deeply social creatures. When we are disconnected from other people we wither and dry up. When I watched the story of Kalief Browder on Netflix, I learned that solitary confinement beyond fifteen days is considered torture by human rights organizations. From this realization and my own experience in the global quarantine, I've developed new compassion for those who are shut-in. At the beginning of the pandemic I stayed indoors as much as I could, but after a month I started to feel truly unsettled. I was locked in under the best of circumstances: a cute apartment with my daughter, my dog, a full fridge, a nice patio, and plenty of phone calls and Zoom parties with friends and family. I can't even imagine what it's like to have no human (or even animal) interaction.

Whether you consider yourself an introvert, extrovert or somewhere in between, we all need connection.

In my twenties I often felt like I was blowing in the wind without an anchor. I knew I didn't believe in the god of my youth. I claimed atheism but didn't have anything to nourish my spirit. I spent time with friends, partied and pursued cocktails. I worked out feverishly to look like a model, often running in place on a treadmill while looking out the window or watching TV. I searched for Mr. Right without having a good sense of who I was. I was successful on paper, working a cushy job with lots of perks and a six-figure salary. When I thought it was time, I married a man, bought a house and had a child. All in order. All part of the dream. Of course, with time, things fell apart as they should when you marry someone on someone else's schedule. We wanted different things. We never really understood each other. After four years, we divorced.

My daughter was only six years old when I relocated to Atlanta. There were many times I was on the verge of completely losing my mind, but one wise decision made all the difference in the world. I recognized that I couldn't make it on my own. Perhaps the same part of me that began a spiritual journey about eight years prior had developed some wisdom. I knew I needed divinity then. Now I knew I needed a village.

I moved to Atlanta on Saturday. The next day I attended an African Methodist Episcopal (AME) church that had been recommended to me. I knew I couldn't be a single mom in a new city without spiritual support and encouragement. In the span of a year I found a psychologist and a massage therapist, as well as the usual doctor and dentist. Joining clubs was harder than I thought it would be – not everyone wanted me. I joined the organizations that were welcoming – the PTA, Atlanta

Track Club, Toastmasters, even the Junior League. I connected with other moms and engaged and nurtured my old friendships from back home. I leaned on my family. I created my village.

Eventually I discovered meetup.com and began creating my own groups. Now I organize three groups on their platform. Technology allowed me to design my support network in an even more meaningful way.

Even with all of that, single parenting in the often-racist south, at times, knocked me off my equilibrium. I've had episodes of depression and grief that have felt like mini breakdowns. I've taken Benadryl in the morning and curled back up in my bed waiting for a painful day to pass me by. If I didn't create a village of support, I fear a day or two in bed would have turned into a week or two, or a month or two, or a visit to a psych ward.

Before becoming a parent, I heard stories about mothers who lost their way, and I could never understand it. The pressure of being the sole provider for another little human broke open my heart and my knowledge. It all made sense now. I just had to make sure not to fall prey to the enormous weight of social responsibility and judgment that comes with being a parent, particularly one that's single.

There's a quote from an old Dramatics song called "Do What You Wanna Do" that always stuck in my head. "The strong give up and move on. The weak give up and stay." I'm thankful that when situations grew from somewhat unhealthy to intensely oppressive, I was able to give up and move on. I suffered and buried myself deep at times, but I didn't get stuck. I didn't stay. I believe my ability to resurface from grief and depression was because I had someone counting on me. I had friends looking for me, and I had a community depending on me. I was also lucky.

Depression can be more than just needing a village. However, it's also more than just needing a pill.

A few times a year, I have had the privilege of gathering around an open fire with a group of friends at a local sweat lodge and committing to support each other as a community. A friend from my meetup group invited me for my first visit in 2016. I had no idea what to expect. The only thing I knew about sweat lodges was the devastating disaster in Arizona in 2009 where three people died.[1]

This experience was the complete opposite. It was beautiful, and I felt safe. I followed my friend down a gently winding trail, lush with greenery, past a tiny pond and through a small makeshift curtain. I could hear the crackle of the fire pit as I approached. Once inside, I saw delicate bamboo mats covering the soft grass, a wooden hut that housed the sauna, picnic tables with water, and small woven baskets containing little slips of paper. I was immediately welcomed by our local guru, a mahogany-skinned brother with long dreads named Robert. He swears he's seventy but doesn't look a day over fifty-five. He started our evening by "smudging" us, allowing the fragrant smoke from burning sage to waft along our arms and legs. Sage is known for its cleansing and spiritual nature. Next, he would apply a dab of red clay to our forehead to represent our connection with the earth.

Inside the sauna, he began with safety first; the wooden stove was hot, very hot, and we were free to go out into the open air whenever we wanted. From there, he led us in spiritual songs and gave us the opportunity to share our struggles and our wisdom with each other. He encouraged us with affirmations, and wouldn't allow us to go home without hugging our fellow participants at least once to share "heart energy." We relaxed on bamboo mats during the breaks between each 5-10 minute session in the sauna. If we desired, we wrote our negative emotions on the papers provided and quietly watched them burn in the fire. As a Brooklyn girl, I didn't have much experience with fire pits. I found it completely mesmerizing. My mind settled thoroughly as my eyes followed the dancing embers.

At the end of the evening, our group of about a dozen people would leave having experienced the physical benefits of the sauna, but also the emotional benefits of community. Like so many things in life, sweat lodge came to a close in 2020. The space was reclaimed by the land trust that owns the property. I pray that we find a new location for this type of community building and support. The Native Americans who began this tradition had it right. Our ancestors had it right. Gathering around a fire is deeply communal. Being in nature is incredibly grounding. Sweating out toxins is exceptionally freeing. Having all of these experiences together is profoundly intoxicating. Not many people have such a wonderful opportunity.

The magic of transformative experiences increases exponentially when we are in community.

American society is structured in a way that makes many of us feel lonely. We have individual goals and often live alone. Media and advertising encourage us to compete with our neighbors and keep up with the Joneses. We compare our homes, work, clothes, cars, relationships, and even where our kids go to school. The labyrinth isn't as easy as it appears from far away – even some support groups are notorious for offering more competition than actual help.

It's not easy to create your village – it requires authenticity and effort. My daughter is now a happy, well-adjusted college student. We sailed through her teenage years and our friendship is strong. Being a parent is a Herculean job – being a successful single parent requires Divine intervention. Whether you are a parent or not, we all need support. Nobody will build your village for you. You have to throw up the plyboards yourself.

Affirmations for Connection:
- I bring my unique and valuable experiences to every group I'm in.
- Asking for help is a sign of courage and confidence.
- I am generous and enjoy helping others.
    (Repeat at least 2x per day.)

Reflection Questions:
- How would you describe the growth or change in your personal and community network in the past few years?
- How might you build on your personal network based on your interests and belief systems?
- Are you happy with the level of support and connection in your life?

Time to Get Still:
- Visit TrishAhjelRoberts.com/resources and access Meditation #3 for Connection.
    (Enjoy at least 2x per week, but daily is ideal.)

Let's Pollinate!
Make a commitment to identify groups, networks and activities that interest you. I encourage you to consider some of these categories:
- Charitable (local and national non-profits, social justice organizations, food banks, etc.) This is first because it's the most important. Helping others is empowering and makes you a better and happier person.
- Physical (fitness center, YMCA, yoga studio, etc.)
- Spiritual (church, temple, meditation center, mosque, ashram, etc.)
- Affinity (LGBTQ, vegan, Caribbean, girls' night out, Black moms, etc.)
- Hobby (walking, knitting, dancing, card games, etc.)
- Intellectual (discussion groups, book clubs, career or personal development, leadership, political, etc.)

- ❖ Set a SMART goal: Specific, Measurable, Attainable, emotionally Relevant and Timebound.
- ❖ Continue to work with your accountability partner.

Grooves for Fluttering:
- ❖ Bill Withers. "Lean on Me." *Still Bill*, 1972.
- ❖ Cece Winans and Whitney Houston. "Count on Me." *Waiting to Exhale*, 1995.
- ❖ Inner Life. "Ain't No Mountain High Enough." Salsoul Records, vinyl, 1981.
- ❖ Fire Island featuring Marc Anthoni. "If You Should Need a Friend." Junior Boy's Own, vinyl, 1995.

Think-Through Films:
- ❖ *Hidden Figures*. Directed by Theodore Melfi. Starring Taraji P. Henson and Octavia Spencer. Fox 2000 Pictures, 2017.
- ❖ *Avatar*. Directed by James Cameron. Starring Sam Worthington and Zoe Saldana. Twentieth Century Fox, 2009.
- ❖ *Moonlight*. Directed by Barry Jenkins. Starring Mahershala Ali. A24, 2016.
- ❖ *Invictus*. Directed by Clint Eastwood. Starring Morgan Freeman and Matt Damon. Liberty Pictures, 2009.
- ❖ *Time: The Kalief Browder Story*. Directed by Jenner Furst. Documentary. Roc Nation Production, 2020.

Additional Resources:
- ❖ TrishAhjelRoberts.com/resources is your main portal for all resources.
- ❖ Meetup.com is my favorite resource for finding groups of like-minded folks. Don't give up if the first one you try doesn't work out.
- ❖ Facebook groups and events are also very good. Learn your privacy settings and block or unfollow anyone who unsettles your spirit.
- ❖ Amazon, Audible, Google, YouTube and your local library

Fourth Drop: Get REAL with Someone

> "To be authentic is the highest form of praise. You're fulfilling your mission and purpose on earth when you honor the real you."
> - Oprah Winfrey

_____
_____
_____
_____

So, you've healed a bit, or at least acknowledged past hurts and noticed a few band-aids. You've claimed your inner spirit and started building a support network. Now it's time to get REAL.

When I was a kid my father used to say, "You have to know who you are." It sounded wise, but I didn't know what he was talking about – I had no idea who I was. I knew the biggest limbs of my family tree and the sequence of my resume. I knew what I did for fun and the religion I was taught. I knew the gender, race and nationality that was ascribed to me. *Was I the manifestation of that data?*

The New Oxford dictionary defines self-awareness as "conscious knowledge of one's own character, feelings, motives and desires." I have encountered many articles and memes about self-love and self-care, but I can't recall any about self-awareness. It seems impossible to love yourself or others authentically if you don't know yourself well.

Trying to cultivate self-love without self-awareness is like slicing bread before it's baked.

I know we can experience some level of self-love without knowing ourselves well. Perhaps a more perfunctory form, the same way abused children still love their parents. We might love ourselves because we feel we have no choice.

Self-development helps us to authentically love ourselves because we grow our desired qualities while reprogramming false messages.

You can live an entire lifetime without self-awareness. My guess is many people who've experienced trauma either physically or emotionally may not want to know themselves too well, because of the pain inherent in unearthing the realities of the past. That's why the first drop is "Heal the Past First." I would argue that all Black women in the U.S. suffer from race-based trauma as a result of living in a country that doesn't value us. We have been largely left out of the history and beauty standards of the land of our birth. We are stereotyped as oversexed, undereducated, angry and loud.

So how do we become self-aware? The fact that you're reading this book shows that you are one of the curious few who wants a more authentic, joyful and inspired life. It's never too late to begin or deepen a journey of self-awareness. Turns out my dad was right about knowing who you are, and by working through this book, you are well on the path.

Many of us go through our lives feeling like there's something not quite right with us. We might feel insecure about our parents or neighborhood. Maybe we were physically, sexually or verbally abused. Perhaps we grew up in poverty. We could have been betrayed by people who were supposed to love us – family, partners or friends. Maybe we were victims of media messages about how we should look, where we should live, who we should love and how much we should own.

I remember when I was in elementary school in Crown Heights, Brooklyn, a classmate asked if my hair was real. I explained my mom put "that cream" in it with a combination of embarrassment and pride. I didn't have what we used to call "good" hair like a Puerto Rican, but it was long and straight with my relaxer. It was a desirable look for a little Black girl in those days. That was before weaves and colored contacts came out in the '80s. Black women have been presented with every possible type of hair straightener, skin lightener, colored contacts and Brazilian hair on a platter next to self-doubt, self-loathing and insecurity. Despite the fact that our bodies are stereotyped as naturally curvy, breast and butt implants have become increasingly common. I want my Black sisters to be as joyful with a weave as a bald head. To feel as beautiful in designer brands as in bare skin. To feel sexy with a big or little booty, A cups or D's, and a tiny or full waist. I know it's aspirational, but every action is born of an idea. Just imagine naked, bald-headed you, walking with pride as Maya Angelou famously penned in her poem, "Still I Rise," like you had "diamonds at the meeting of (your) thighs."

Now, I know we're not all going to shave our heads, drop our clothes and walk boldly into our barefooted future, and I'm not saying you don't have the right to adorn or augment yourself in whatever way makes you feel most beautiful. However, wherever you are on the spectrum, we can work on getting as real and honest with ourselves as we can be inside and out.

Beauty is in our quirky and unique flaws and imperfections. It's is in our ability to delight in our features unapologetically. We can't be genuinely happy if we can't be ourselves inside and out. There's no more striking combination than authenticity and confidence.

I shaved my head nearly bald in 1989 when I was twenty-one. After a few months of wearing a Salt-n-Pepa bob, I realized I liked the hair at the nape of my neck, and I couldn't remember ever seeing it before. (I had a relaxer since the age of eight.) Back in those days I thought all Black people had the same hair texture. Now we have a whole classification system for the coil or kink of our hair. At the time, I just wanted to experience my natural hair. It was refreshing! The breeze blew and the sun shone on my scalp. My dandruff disappeared. (I learned later that relaxers really harmed my scalp.) I stayed mostly natural for the rest of my life until I moved to the south in 2007. I worried about getting a job with my natural hair. It wasn't until my mom died of breast cancer in 2011 that I gave up relaxers completely. The first time I cut out my relaxer was for fun and self-awareness; the second time was for my health. The fact of the matter is, they're toxic and anything that is applied to the skin enters the bloodstream. The southern corporate world would just have to deal with me and my natural tresses.

Society teaches us that we need a particular image for some roles and a different façade for others. We are not taught to be our whole and complete selves as we move between various spaces – work, home, school, relationships, etc. We wonder what box we should fit into, and why we need a box anyway. I think that's why so many of us struggle with authenticity. Hair is just a manifestation. Is it okay to be ourselves with our unique beauty and blemishes, or do we need to meet other's perceptions of who we should be? Do we need the Indian hair, acrylic nails and false eyelashes to be beautiful or even socially acceptable? Do we have to go to church on Sundays, watch football, or eat chicken wings and go out for cocktails after work when we really don't want to? How many ways do we mask our true selves to fit in?

I believe we are facing a national crisis of authenticity. We are so obsessed with perfection, that at the end of a day of social media and other filters, many of us feel unrecognizable to ourselves and deeply alone. Up until about ten years ago, I used to wear foundation every day. Then, one day I inadvertently skipped it, and someone commented on how beautiful my skin was. *Are you fucking kidding me?* I wonder how many other ways that happens to us – we put on a mask that we think is beautiful and the real beauty lies in the imperfections beneath. In the natural curl or kink of our hair – the puffy, fuzzy and nappy. In our freckles or moles. In our scars and the complicated stories they tell. I can't count the number of times I've seen women with bad weaves and beautiful faces, or too much makeup and huge eyelashes shading the window to gorgeous, big brown eyes.

I encourage you to consider your own masks. Are they physical like makeup, hair or nails? Or subtle like building emotional walls to reduce the opportunity to create meaningful relationships? Or profound like holding on to secrets that absolutely nobody knows? (For the record, therapists are sworn to confidentiality if you don't trust anyone you know.)

I know I'm biased, but I think natural Black women are *the* most beautiful. For some reason, I always have. I love our African hair and features. I know the dominant white culture, and often, Black men, don't validate our natural beauty. Black men are also victims of the ubiquitous "white is right" mentality. I'm not here to tell anyone to get rid of nails, weaves or makeup, just recognize a mask for what it is. Some masks are functional – they may camouflage us or keep us warm. If you choose to wear one, that's fine.

If you want to be authentic
you should at least be aware of your masks.
That self-awareness is the path to authenticity
and self-love.

For most of my life I worked in corporate America and wore a suit jacket, understated makeup, appropriate jewelry and conservatively manicured nails. When I became self-employed, I had to figure out what I wanted to wear after so many years of donning the corporate uniform. For women on television, full makeup, weaves and eyelashes may be part of the uniform. For doctors it may be your white coat. For healthcare workers it may be your smock or your scrubs. You may not want or need to throw out the uniform, but understand you are not your uniform. You are not your mask.

Your identity and self-worth arise from your humanity and your Divine consciousness – not your role or outward appearance.

The process of self-reflection and unearthing can be awkward, but the reward is so deep and juicy it's worth the effort. REAL connection, support and love is resounding and priceless. You can never have those things when you show up in the world as anything less than your most authentic, beautifully flawed and truest self. Whoopi Goldberg and Maya Angelou strike me as examples of women who showed up in the world as themselves and found huge success. Of course, there are many more. I remember when Oprah Winfrey went on TV with no makeup and people had a lot to say about it. That's part of her success. She's been real with us all along. Even Cardi B came on the scene with every ounce of her Bronx attitude intact and an outrageous sense of humor, and all sixty-nine million of us fell in love and follow her on Instagram. Michelle Obama has forty million followers. She's another glowing example of authenticity. I was shocked by how much she shared in *Becoming*, but it only made me admire her more.

People are flawed and that's real. When we seem a little too perfect, we either worked through our shit or we're faking it. You may not want the world to know all your problems, but at least one person needs to know your crazy-ass, imperfect self. Lol! No one's perfect, and we can't work through our issues if we can't take a good look at ourselves. We need at least one ear for validation – because you are not the only one with issues, and you need to know that. What you don't want is to start lying to everyone about who you actually are and slip into a place of loneliness where the only one who really knows you is your cat. In her song, "Get it Together," India Arie wisely sings, "The words that come from your mouth you're the first to hear." When we lie to others, we lie to ourselves first. When we lie to ourselves, we lose who we are and wander the streets as plastic zombies lost, trying to remember the way home.

From a place of authenticity, true friendships can be born. I feel so blessed to have friends who know my idiosyncrasies and shortcomings as well as my talents and strengths. I've lost many "friends" over the years, and I'm sure I will lose more. Most of us will. Some people were never my friends – they were acquaintances, drinking buddies, moms from school, coworkers and classmates. They were in my life for a season. Very few stay the course. If you're lucky enough to foster the ride-or-die variety, treat them like gold. Friendships are an essential part of sanity. They nurture the spirit and the soul, and they restore our belief in others in a world that is so often unspeakable.

This doesn't mean that just because you have a friend who's been around since elementary school, they can abuse you with toxic conversations that diminish you, betrayal or other types of abuse. Michelle Obama has a powerful quote in her memoir *Becoming*, "Walk away from friendships that make you feel small and insecure and seek out people who inspire you and support you." Sometimes even the oldest of friendships need to be released if they get in the way of our personal development and healing. It doesn't mean your friends have to be on a path identical to yours, but if they are crabs trying to pull you back into the barrel, you have to take inventory. You may circle back to each other when the timing is right. When we're real with ourselves we have to be real with others too. We teach people how to treat us by our actions, even if that means letting go. This release creates space. In Michelle's example, it makes room for "people who inspire and support you."

We only have twenty-four hours in a day.
If we want authentic, elevated friendships
we need to make room for them.

Honest, loving friendships are profoundly important for emotional and physical well-being. It matters who you spend your time with. You exchange not only words, jokes and information, but energy. I've had conversations with so-called friends that have left me drained and upset, and others that have left me inspired and uplifted. I choose the latter when I can. Without authenticity, you don't have a friend you just have "someone you know."

When you begin paying attention and qualifying friendships differently, you may find that you want to cultivate new friendships. As you heal and create community as recommended in the first and second drops, you will encounter new seeds of friendship. It's up to you if you decide to nurture them.

Strong friendships are born from knowledge of each other over time. I've narrowed friendship to a few basic elements: shared experiences, reliability, authenticity, vulnerability, trust, non-judgmental listening, optimism, helpfulness and commitment of time. For long-term friendships there must be humility, as well, because sometimes we hurt each other and must apologize and make amends.

We trust our close friends and partners with our hearts. We show up with them as our true and flawed selves. Getting real is about figuring out who you are, accepting it and sharing yourself cautiously and appropriately with folks who deserve you. Getting real is the first yellow brick on the road to happiness and fulfillment. You can't skip over it. Spending time here reaps one of the most sought-out rewards – genuine, honest and unshakeable self-love. When you love yourself, you speak kindly to yourself. You have patience with yourself. You forgive yourself. You don't harm yourself. You don't feel guilty about your choices. You treat yourself like a well-loved newborn baby – with all the sweetness, care and attention you deserve.

Affirmations for Self-Love:
- I am intelligent. I am beautiful. I am more than enough.
- Today I choose to love me exactly as I am.
- The world wants to meet my flawed, authentic self. Real is beautiful.

    (Repeat at least 2x per day.)

Reflection Questions:
- What physical and emotional masks do you wear and why?
- Do you feel like you need to work on self-awareness, self-love or authenticity?
- Is not being REAL holding you back?

Time to Get Still:
- Visit TrishAhjelRoberts.com/resources and access Meditation #4 for Self-Love.

    (Try for at least 2x per week, but daily is ideal.)

Let's Pollinate!
- Make a commitment to pursue self-awareness, self-love and authenticity. You might want to stop telling little white lies or really big lies. Maybe you want to read autobiographies with difficult truths. You might want to work on developing qualities you're proud of to give you more honest conversation. I've listed some books I've found helpful.
- Set a SMART goal: Specific, Measurable, Attainable, emotionally Relevant and Timebound. Continue to work with your accountability partner.

Grooves for Fluttering:
- Janelle Monáe. "I Like That." *I Like That*, 2018.
- Alicia Keys. "Girl on Fire." *Girl on Fire*, 2012.
- Sade. "Soldier of Love." *Soldier of Love,* 2009.
- Whitney Houston. "Greatest Love of All." *Whitney Houston*, 1985.
- India Arie. "Get it Together." *Voyage to India*, 2002.

Think-Through Films:
- *Becoming*. Directed by Nadia Hallgren. Starring Michelle Obama. Higher Ground Productions, 2020.
- *Their Eyes Were Watching God*. Directed by Darnell Martin. Starring Halle Berry and Michael Ealy. Harpo Films, 2005.
- *Nappily Ever After*. Directed by Haifaa al-Mansour. Starring Sanaa Lathan. Netflix, 2018
- *Back to Natural*. Directed by Gillian Scott-Ward, PhD. Starring Salamisha Tillet. Dominic Ward Production, 2019.

Additional Resources:
- TrishAhjelRoberts.com/resources is your main portal for all resources.
- *I Know Why the Caged Bird Sings* by Maya Angelou
- *We're Going to Need More Wine* by Gabrielle Union
- *Becoming* by Michelle Obama
- *And Still I Rise: A Book of Poems* by Maya Angelou
- Amazon, Audible, Google, YouTube and your local library

Fifth Drop: Anger is a Lie

"Exaggeration is truth that has lost its temper."
 - Kahlil Gibran

_____
_____
_____
_____

If you've worked your way through the first four drops, congratulations! You're on your way to a life of joy and fulfillment like you've never experienced before – rich with healing, spirituality, community and authenticity. If you've made time for meditation and daily affirmations, you should already be feeling a shift in your consciousness. Maybe you've even had a few *aha!* moments along the way.

Now let's get into one of my favorite and most misunderstood topics – anger. I used to think anger was a necessary evil, an unavoidable emotion. I had no choice but to respond with anger to injustice, insult or injury. In my mind it was an emotion as valid as love, joy, fear or pain. I remember reading an article many years ago, probably around 2000, that said anger wasn't a real emotion, but rather a way of masking genuine feelings. Interesting. I put that in my back pocket and forgot it in the wash.

Years later, in 2010, I went to my first meditation session hoping to settle my spirit – neither my job nor my relationship was working out, single parenting was bringing me to my knees. I was deeply exhausted, hurt and angry. I was angry with the subtle and overt racism I'd slowly come to recognize as a thread throughout my entire life. Angry that a beautiful, kind, educated young woman like me couldn't find an appropriate partner. Angry that even with my MBA and an impressive job title, I didn't make enough money as a financial advisor to comfortably support myself and my daughter without help from my parents. Angry that I had to sit in meetings with affluent clients offering my investment expertise while I didn't have enough money of my own to invest in anything. Angry that my reality made me feel like a hypocrite through no fault of my own. I was working full-time and receiving assistance the same as any cafeteria worker, school bus driver or Walmart employee might. I had become the stereotypical "angry Black woman." I was her and she was me. You might not have known by looking at me. I still walked around with a smile, but below the surface there was a constant simmer. I was tired of jumping hurdles that got raised each year while my paycheck remained the same. I was exhausted from trying to fit into spaces that would never accept me. The pain was deep, and anger seemed to give it a much-needed outlet.

 Since then, I learned to see anger for what it is: a negative exaggeration of reality. You don't have to be Buddhist to appreciate this wisdom any more than you have to be Christian to honor the ten commandments. When you're angry with someone you highlight their negative characteristics and downplay their good qualities. Suddenly your loved one is transformed into a mean and terrible person through the lens of your anger. You can't honestly see the whole person anymore. The same can be said for institutions or other objects of our anger. That's why you sometimes hear the expression "blind rage." However, there are consequences – High blood pressure. War. Injury. Unhappiness. Stroke. Ulcer. Disease. Anger is tricky like that. It makes you think it's helping you – smiling in your face and offering release, when meanwhile it's pickpocketing you – destroying your internal organs and your peace of mind.

    Have you ever tried to have a conversation with someone who is angry about something that happened many years ago? I once had a client who said someone stole money from him in a business transaction and he would never stop fighting to get it back. He was proud of his determination and prepared to go to the police, to court, and to the newspaper, fully willing to spend the next ten years making sure the scammer didn't "get away" with it. I told him sometimes you've got to reclaim your life. Don't let the person who harmed you take the next ten years too.

    I remember hearing my own screams in 2018 as the back of my VW Beetle was hit by a tractor trailer at highway speed. My new car was totaled, and I could have easily died. Time seemed to slow down as the huge grill of the truck pressed against my driver's side window and pushed me along the highway. The driver lied to the police and said I was trying to change lanes. He wasn't given a ticket, so there was no determination of fault. When I got over the initial shock and was back home, my first instinct was to be angry with the driver for lying about something so important. I took a deep breath and tried to put myself in his shoes. With missing front teeth and a confederate flag on his baseball cap, my guess was he didn't have a good education or access to quality medical care. I could have assumed he was racist, but I was far enough along in my own journey to know that anger wouldn't help even if he were. I believe racism stems from sadness and ignorance, so when I encounter obviously racist people, I feel outrage and pity simultaneously.

    I decided to go deeper – maybe the perpetrator needed the gift of my grace. Like most people, I've done things over the course of my life that could have gone south. I've been the grateful recipient of the adage, "God looks out for fools and babies." Maybe it was time to give the gift of grace to someone else. I imagined the driver needed his job so much he had to decide between honesty and survival. Maybe he needed some grace. And for me, that car accident felt like a message from the Universe to change course. I wrote about it on my fifty-first birthday in my Wellness & Transformation Blog (honeybutterflyz.com/blog) on September 10, 2019 in a post entitled, "A Hard Left Turn." That accident was the catalyst for a whole lot of soul-searching. *What did the Universe want from me? If I was supposed to die, I would have.*

At the time, my daughter was on a study-abroad trip in France. *Was I supposed to move to France?* A few months later, I changed jobs. *Was that the lesson?* I embarked on a quest which drove me to step out with faith and courage. It was from this place that I launched my dream business, HoneyButterflyz Wellness & Transformation, and created the book you're reading now. If that truck hadn't hit me, I wonder if I'd still be working as an underpaid financial advisor with a closetful of unused talents. By releasing myself from the anger and reframing it, I was able to get on with my life and spread wings, gliding on the knowledge that even the darkest circumstances provide opportunity for growth.

***It's often in our most difficult experiences that we find the uncut diamonds,
gentle truths and epiphanies
if we muster the strength and courage to look.***

The day after that accident was one of the happiest days of my life. I had been sleepwalking for years, and the hard bang and screeching blare of crumpled metal and burning tires woke me up.

It's always a little funny to me how we all want compassion for ourselves, yet it can be so hard to give to others. I want white people to see, understand and be so outraged by racism that they commit to action. I want men to do the same with sexism. I want cis-gender straight folks to stand up for the LGBTQ community. In reality, people don't pay much attention to other people's dilemmas, and it's hard to understand the circumstances of others. We're just too busy worrying about our own issues. I hope this will open your heart. In order to quell anger and live joyfully, we have to grow our compassion for others. Consider wearing someone else's well-worn Timberlands or downtrodden Converse to gain a whole new perspective. You may want to view yourself as the magnanimous purveyor of grace, or just a regular person who doesn't want to spend the next ten years nurturing an ulcer or arterial plaque. You may want to improve your Karma and advance your spiritual journey, or just sleep well without wine or Ambien.

***Whatever you choose,
you'd be wise to release the anger option.
And yes, it is an option.***

I've had people say we need to get angry to fight injustice. They are right that we absolutely need to fight injustice. However, anger is not the path. It's not any path. I give you Gandhi and Martin Luther King, Jr. Remember the key concept was nonviolence? King's followers went through rigorous training to make sure they didn't lose their tempers and incite violence. I wonder how the movement would have gone if, instead of putting white violence on display, marches had erupted in Black violence? There's not much to wonder about. Had there been a display of Black violence it would have changed the narrative from a righteous civil rights movement to a disorganized race riot. We've seen the scenario play out many times across the U.S., from Los Angeles and Crown Heights to Ferguson.

George Floyd's murder in Minneapolis created a unique and perfect storm in a world on pause from quarantine. His death was so egregious it sparked empathy and outrage from people who would traditionally offer explanations. The clear intent of the officer involved, despite the desperate pleas of onlookers, made this killing of a Black man different from others that had come before. Perhaps, because the world had paused, we were able to clearly see the need for global justice.

The New Oxford American Dictionary defines the "butterfly effect" as "the phenomenon whereby a minute localized change in a complex system can have large effects elsewhere, from the notion in chaos theory that a butterfly fluttering in Rio de Janeiro could change the weather in Chicago."

George Floyd's death created a butterfly effect, but we are all butterflies with the capacity to create massive change though small contributions.

We've all had the opportunity to see the descent into violence and reemergence of focused and coordinated protest. We've seen the remarkable grace of his beautiful family as they passionately called for justice. Anger can most certainly erupt when you take your eyes off the prize. We are all human. However, with a motivated, passionate and focused mind you can go much farther without the distraction of anger.

Even with all the frustration and pain I've described through personal and race-based trauma, I know I've never been an angry person. Happiness and laughter have always been at my core, but there was a time when anger was my lover – a warm shoulder to lay my burdens down at the end of a long day. Not only in its typical manifestations, but in its more subtle varieties: disappointment, annoyance, bitterness, discouragement, impatience. I rested my head on it. I put seasoning on it. I drank wine with it.

Anger allowed me to feel falsely empowered while hiding from my pain and delaying solutions to my problems. It tricked me into believing it was a reliable friend.

Anger rears its head in both small and large ways, but always when we don't get our own way. Traffic should flow for us like we are angels floating on wings. The train should never pass our station. We should never get caught in the rain. That little twinge of impatience, jealousy, discouragement, annoyance. Don't let it fool you, it's all part of the same machine, and the machine is not your friend, even if it shows up with cupcakes and roses.

So how can we reduce our anger?
The first step is to stop believing in it.

When I feel anger rise in my body, my heart races and I can feel the hair on my head start to bristle. I recognize it and I say to myself "not today." I won't be getting high blood pressure today. I won't be making myself miserable today. I will take this breath right here. Right now. In the space of this breath I will evaluate my trigger. In the space of this breath I will choose a different outcome. Stop believing anger is motivating you, encouraging you or fueling your passion. Anger creates an unfocused mind. You can be motivated, encouraged and fueled by love. Martin Luther King Jr. said it best, "Darkness cannot drive out darkness; only light can do that. Hate cannot drive out hate; only love can do that."

Practicing meditation is a powerful way to change your relationship with anger. It helps us recognize the space between action and our response. In that space we can choose our reaction. There are many different types of meditation. I've been practicing Kadampa Buddhist meditation since 2010 and have been teaching since 2016. I'm also trained in a variety of other styles through my yoga training. I find the Kadampa practice to be most helpful, so it's what I incorporate most in the meditation offerings at the end of each chapter. With this style there is plenty of guidance to help redirect your mind when you wander, and, you will always be given an anchor to focus on, whether the breath or some other focal point. Guided visualizations are a powerful way to redirect the mind to a place of positivity. The meditation at the end of this section includes a beautiful visualization to help reduce anger in all its forms – from annoyance, frustration, disappointment and bitterness, to rage and fury.

Anger is the outgrowth of the pain you feel when things don't happen the way you think they should. It's a tumor that needs to be removed.

Once you can identify the space between thought and reaction, give it a try in your everyday life. Traffic or commuting are examples that are easy for most of us to use. You're rushing to an important appointment and you're stuck. You will be late. You feel the anger, annoyance or frustration rising. (It doesn't matter what you call it.) Now use that space between the unwanted delay and your emotional reaction. You can be grateful you're not in a car accident causing the traffic, or the sick passenger causing a train delay. You can be hopeful that this delay is keeping you out of a bad situation you're unaware of. You can accept the fact that you will be late for your meeting and enjoy a few extra minutes of your favorite music, radio show, podcast or audiobook instead. You can mentally wish the people near you a happy and safe journey. All these options are healthier for you and everyone else around you than upsetting yourself. This doesn't mean you can't look for another route if that's possible. You can, and maybe it will work. But if you can't, you can still be happy. Maybe happier because of the unexpected gift of a few more moments to yourself.

Suppose you're in an unhealthy relationship and your partner says something incredibly mean and degrading. Your immediate instinct is to reply in kind or worse. Find the space between the trigger and your response. You don't have to give someone the power to "push your buttons" and control you like an iPhone. *What are your options?* Perhaps acknowledge that this is not the person you want as a partner and just give a knowing nod. Maybe, recognize that they're trying to hurt you and don't fall for it this time. Take some time later to work on your exit strategy or consider couple's therapy. Your partner will find it very hard to fight by themself or to berate someone who doesn't show hurt and pain and rise to their own uncontrolled anger.

Suppose a family member abused you as a child and now you have to see them at Thanksgiving, shouldn't you be angry at them or the family member who invited them? The problem with anger is it doesn't hurt *other* people; it only hurts *you*. You might choose not to participate in the dinner and instead volunteer feeding the homeless or doing something else to elevate your spirit and contribute to the world around you. Whatever you decide, I encourage you to take a stand for yourself. You don't have to be in the presence of an abuser. Attending the family gathering while sitting and stewing or repressing your trauma hurts you and allows the abuser to continue to harm others by not being held accountable. Sometimes we have to love from afar, distancing ourselves from people, even family, who seem either intent or oblivious to our pain.

The examples go on and on. What if someone breaks into your house to harm you, can you defend yourself? Of course. You can kill someone in self-defense without even being angry with them. In a crazy twist, preventing someone from the negative Karma of harming you, actually helps that person. I'm going a little bit deep down the Buddhist rabbit hole here. If you find these Buddhist teachings or "Dharma" interesting, I encourage you to check out kadampa.org for more spiritual goodies. I find the teachings incredibly useful in my everyday life.

Anger itself has no purpose except to blind you from your underlying emotions, damage your physical body and encourage you to make wrong decisions. When you release anger, you will become shocked by how light and beautiful life will become. This doesn't mean you don't stand up for yourself. You just choose your battles wisely and fight with a clear head and a healthy heart.

This doesn't mean that you repress your anger or ignore your emotions. It means that you open the door to work through your real emotions, usually an extremely busy ego coupled with pain.

A simple reverse of Kahlil Gibran's quote gives us, "Temper is truth that has been exaggerated." An exaggeration is a lie. Anger isn't honest. It isn't profound. Its depth is only in its shallowness.

If you still want to be angry and therefore blind, I ask you, do *you* want to be seen as whole? If you want to see others and be seen, anger is the lover you will need to release. If you still want to be angry, I have bad news.

You can't be happy and angry at the same time. You'll be like a butterfly trying to fly with a hornet on its back. Anger can't elevate you. It will buzz in your ear, throw you off course, and weigh you down.

If you're reading this book, I know you want more from life. When anger becomes an insignificant acquaintance instead of a good friend, you'll be ready to soar. This doesn't mean you won't feel the heat of anger rising at times, but with some practice you can identify it, ignore it like green bean casserole at a picnic and work with your true emotions. What a gift! Hold on to your hat and get ready to fly!

Affirmations for Peace:
- I enjoy a life free from anger and the harm it does to me.
- I'm strong enough to recognize and work through my pain.
- I have compassion for others even when it's inconvenient.
  (Repeat at least 2x per day.)

Reflection Questions:
- Have there been times in your life when anger has caused problems in your physical or mental health and relationships?
- Do you still believe that anger is beneficial at times? If so, why?
- Can you imagine a life without anger? If so, do you think you'd be missing out on anything?
- What do you think you might gain by learning to release and reframe your anger?

Time to Get Still:
- Visit TrishAhjelRoberts.com/resources and access Meditation #5 for Peace.
  (Try for at least 2x per week, but daily is ideal.)

Let's Pollinate!
- Make a commitment to pursue a calmer, lighter life in the absence of anger.
- Set a SMART goal: Specific, Measurable, Attainable, emotionally Relevant and Timebound.
- Continue to work with your accountability partner.

Grooves for Fluttering:
- Donald Glover. "This is America." *This is America,* 2018.
- Bob Marley. "Redemption Song." *Uprising,* 1980.
- John Lennon. "Imagine." *Imagine,* 1971.
- Pharrell Williams. "Happy." *Happy,* 2013.

Think-Through Films:
- *Selma.* Directed by Ava DuVernay. Starring David Oyelowo. Pathé Harpo Films, 2014.
- *Ghandi.* Directed by Richard Attenborough. Starring Ben Kingsley. Goldcrest Films, 1982.
- *A Bold Peace.* Directed by Matthew Eddy. Documentary. Bullfrog Films, 2016.

Additional Resources:
- TrishAhjelRoberts.com/resources is your main portal for all resources.
- *Universal Compassion* by Geshe Kelsang Gyatso
- *Thoughts on Everything.* Blog. Trish Ahjel Roberts HoneyButterflyz.com/blog.
- Kadampa.org
- Amazon, Audible, Google, YouTube and your local library

Sixth Drop: Give it Away for Free

> "If you only have one smile in you,
> give it to the people you love."
> - Maya Angelou

_____
_____
_____
_____

You are glowing. You are radiant. You are healing yourself and connecting to your internal goddess and the community. You're showing up unapologetically YOU in ways you never have before. You emanate fiery passion while inside you're soft and peaceful, like a newborn baby. Face it, you're the B.O.M.B. Now what good is all that fabulousness if you're not willing to share?

I consider myself a giver. I organized the Black Vegan Life™ meetup group in Atlanta for three years before asking members to chip in with a membership fee, and that was only because I really needed the coins. (It's available for free again, so check us out.) I published my novel, *Chocolate Soufflé,* as a love letter to my mother and myself without giving any thought to commercial success. I give hugs and encouragement with wild abandon. (Well, before COVID-19 anyway. Now I just give the encouragement.) I offer my help, when I can, and I'm delighted when I can inspire folks. I'm 100% certain that every ounce of positive energy and tangible items I've given away have or will come back to me many times over.

One of the first books I read with my Black Vegan Life™ meetup group was *Super Rich* by Russell Simmons back in 2015. He was not the flashy and shallow hip-hop mogul I feared he might be, but rather a deep, thoughtful brother, long-time vegan, animal rights advocate and yogi. In his book he talked about the early years of his career when he created mixed tapes with seminal artists like Run DMC and LL Cool J, and instead of trying to sell them, he gave them to DJs around New York City for free in the hopes that his music would get heard. Once people experienced his talent and that of the artists he produced, they wanted more. He had a following long before the concept of a social media following existed. This initial leap of faith – giving away talent for free – was the secret weapon.

He really made me think about my manuscript for *Chocolate Soufflé*, which had been sitting in a manila envelope since the '90s. He made me question my other talents. Was I holding anything so close to my chest that it wasn't serving me or the planet? What's the point of having a gift, if I'm not willing to share it? How would my light ever shine if I sat quietly in a closet being a good girl and keeping all boats unrocked?

We live in a society that teaches us we should be paid for our efforts, that values wealth above all else, and that glorifies the misery of the grind. Someone sold us the narrative that if we work ourselves into exhaustion, cognitive dissonance, poor health and moral dilemmas, we'll achieve Nirvana. I started my first full-time job at a corporation when I was only seventeen. I worked at more than five Fortune 100 companies and a few non-profits. I can't count the number of times I've had to make an unpopular decision to keep from sliding down the ethical slippery slope, or the innumerable times I prioritized my family, my health or my joy. I have seen many others cave in to ethical pressures to their reward or demise. I've seen folks work themselves into sickness and sadness despite monetary wealth.

What would the world look like if people shared their talents freely? Imagine all the art, songs, inventions, music and ideas we've missed out on because someone took their talent to the grave. Now close your eyes and imagine the opposite – a world where everyone is self-actualized, including you. Take a moment to dream a world without barriers to basic necessities like food and safe housing – a society where all children got a quality education that included an honest history of their country, ethnicity and identity. Imagine we birthed a culture of lawyers who enjoy advocacy, police who enjoy protecting, doctors who enjoy healing, janitors who enjoy cleaning, waiters who enjoy serving, politicians who enjoy representing, executives who enjoy leading and construction workers who enjoy building. It seems crazy, but as Nelson Mandela said, "It always seems impossible until it's done."

In the late '80s I worked at a major financial institution at the World Financial Center in downtown NYC. (The WFC and Winter Garden Atrium appear in the classic movie Boomerang, if you are in the mood for a throwback.) The mail room staff was comprised of mentally disabled people. They seemed so excited and challenged by their work. This same job given to someone with a higher mental capacity would have been exceptionally frustrating, even demeaning. From where I sat, the mail room staff was self-actualized.

I wish I could say I always had this concept wrapped up in my mind with a neat little bow. The reality is, I came frighteningly close to keeping every drop of my own talent to myself. When I first wrote *Chocolate Soufflé* back in 1995, I shopped it with publishers and couldn't find any takers. I let that rejection silence me because, if I couldn't get *paid,* why *write?* My Black Vegan Life™ community encouraged me to publish my novel in 2015. I spent my own money and I did it for love. We spend money on clothes and on vacations. Why not invest in our own dreams and talents? Whether you love or hate the book, it's my creation, crafted through the lens of my own experiences. It's available for anyone to read thanks to the magic of Amazon. I did it for love. I love that I did it. So, if you want to grow, produce, explode, whatever, you first have to put your gifts out into the world.

> *I will not die with my talents,*
> *and neither should you.*
> *I wonder how many people die with their best talents*
> *inside themselves because they refuse*
> *to give anything away for free.*

I can't imagine anyone seeing a benefit to dying with unused, unshared, dusty-ass talents. One of my favorite movies of all times is *Love Jones*. There's a scene where Nia Long's character is about to read her poem. When she doesn't see her love interest in the room, she says, "I guess I'll get it out anyway." In the film, she's a photographer who writes poems for fun. She finds a venue to release her talent whether she was going to profit from it or not. It was an emotional release for her, but also an artistic gift for others at the open mic night. Who knows who might have been changed by her offering?

> *If we're not here to share our gifts, what are we here for?*
> *It can't be to work hard for someone else's dream,*
> *hoard cash and die without identifying, honing or*
> *sharing our natural abilities.*

What you have to offer won't be for everyone. You might have a mind for numbers, a voice for song or hands for carpentry. Perhaps art, music or athleticism are in your soul. We all have talents that only we can share in our unique way. If you're not sure what yours are, I encourage you to begin the excavation.

Identifying your talents and sharing them will renew your sense of vitality, joy and freedom. Most of us will not be in a position to immediately share our passions with the world as our primary occupation. Perhaps you begin with volunteering or hobbies. I stopped writing for twenty years. I had to experience that profound loss of time in order to climb the rafters and ring the bell for YOU. Time flies fast when we're doing other things. Don't miss out on identifying and sharing your passions with a world that's waiting for you.

Be prepared for rejection, but let it make you stronger. Michael Jordan was kicked off his high school basketball team. Mark Zuckerberg started Facebook because he was socially awkward. Jack Canfield, author of the *Chicken Soup for the Soul* books was rejected by 144 publishers before finding the right one.

> ***Just keep offering the best you have***
> ***directly from your heart.***
> ***You won't have to wait for the magic,***
> ***it will ignite spontaneously in you,***
> ***and the world will sigh in gratitude.***

Affirmations for Generosity:
- ❖ I am uniquely talented. I have gifts to offer the world.
- ❖ Nobody can tell my story but me.
- ❖ I will learn and grow by sharing what only I know.

  (Repeat at least 2x per day.)

Reflection Questions:
- ❖ What do you most enjoy doing or what talents do you possess that you would do even without getting paid?
- ❖ How can others benefit from your knowledge or your personal story?
- ❖ How do you feel about your current level of generosity? Remember, you can give a kind word or a "like" on social media. Not everything requires money.

Time to Get Still:
- ❖ Visit TrishAhjelRoberts.com/resources and access Meditation #6 for Generosity.

  (Try for at least 2x per week, but daily is ideal.)

Let's Pollinate!
- ❖ Make a commitment to share your talent, gifts or time with the world.
- ❖ Set a SMART goal: Specific, Measurable. Attainable, emotionally Relevant and Timebound.
- ❖ Continue to work with your accountability partner.

Grooves for Fluttering:
- ❖ Red Hot Chili Peppers. "Give It Away." *Blood Sugar Sex Magik,* 1991.
- ❖ Chaka Khan. "I'm Every Woman." *Chaka,* 1978.
- ❖ Aretha Franklin. "I Say a Little Prayer." *Aretha Now,* 1968.
- ❖ Denroy Morgan. "I'll Do Anything for You." *I'll Do Anything for You,* 1981.

Think-Through Films:
- *Love Jones.* Directed by Theodore Witcher. Starring Nia Long and Larenz Tate. New Line Cinema, 1997.
- *Seven Pounds.* Directed by Gabriele Muccino. Starring Will Smith. Columbia Pictures, 2008.
- *Pay It Forward.* Directed by Mimi Leder. Starring Helen Hunt and Kevin Spacey. Bel-Air Entertainment, 2000.

Additional Resources:
- TrishAhjelRoberts.com/resources is your main portal for all resources.
- *Super Rich* by Russell Simmons
- Meetup.com/Black-vegan-life
- *Boomerang.* Directed by Reginald Hudlin. Starring Eddie Murphy. Imagine Entertainment, 1992.
- Amazon, Audible, Google, YouTube and your local library

Seventh Drop: No More Bag Lady

"I freed a thousand slaves.
I could have freed a thousand more
if only they knew they were slaves."
- Harriet Tubman

_____
_____
_____
_____

In astrology, seven is the number of completion. In the Old Testament, God created the world in seven days. In Vegas, lucky number seven rules. And here we are together, beginning the seventh drop, embarking on the second half of your journey with me. I hope you can feel the shifts within you as you heal, grow spiritually, build community, reduce anger, grow generosity and learn to love yourself authentically. Now it's time to look at the people and things that might be holding us back, and make sure we're not keeping others from soaring.

***Everything around us, especially people, are temporary.
We cause ourselves and others pain
when we get too attached.***

When I moved into my first house in January 2001 with a husband and one-month-old baby, life wasn't perfect, but it was going according to plan. I had a six-figure job, a pretty amazing wardrobe, a handsome husband and a beautiful baby girl. I had an easy pregnancy and was working from home two days per week after six weeks of maternity leave. I had a family member from Grenada living with us to provide childcare, so I was able to go back to work without worry.

I was blessed in so many ways, but my American Dream fantasy quickly dissolved. When my daughter was only two months old, I remember sitting on my bathroom floor crying at three o'clock in the morning. Her father hadn't come home. For me, it was the last straw on a back that had long been weary. My parents had been married for over forty years at that point, and I was raised with an expectation of fidelity. Now I had a child. It was one thing to make a fool of me, but I couldn't accept this example of a father for my sweet, innocent baby girl. I couldn't live with an unfaithful man, and I didn't want to wait until my daughter was old enough to experience the pain of separation. After a heart-to-heart with my mom, I made the decision to finally take my marriage off life-support.

I loved the two-family home in Georgetown, Brooklyn. I enjoyed taking the two-mile walk to the mall with my daughter, making stops along the way to push her in swings at the playground or buy ice cream off the Mr. Frosty truck. I met with friends for elegant dinners, Broadway plays and family gatherings. My divorce was heartbreak and salvation at the same time. If I had stayed my spirit would have died, and I don't know who I might have become. I let go of what I knew to be unhealthy for all three of us. My husband moved out by July, and we found a new rhythm of co-parenting and weekend visits. Life was still good, then 9/11 happened.

I worked in Two World Trade Center for six years as an account manager at a telecom company. I was getting dressed for work the day after my thirty-third birthday when my girlfriend called to tell me to turn on the news. There had been fires in the towers before, so I didn't think much of it. I shrugged my shoulders and decided to work from home, except for a meeting that I had in lower Manhattan. As I was driving to drop my daughter at my parents' house, my soon-to-be ex-husband called, his voice heavy with concern. A second plane had hit. This was no accident.

I arrived at my childhood home hungry for information to help me understand this new reality. We all sat around the television with our eyes glazed over. I watched with my family in horror as beautiful sunlight from a cloudless summer morning ripped through the mammoth buildings. My daughter snacked comfortably in her high chair, as the surreal images of people jumping to their deaths flashed across the screen. Then, the towers fell. I held my head in my hands, imagining all the lost lives. *I must know a lot of dead people.*

Clouds of thick smoke rose from the rubble. The flicker of early flames became apparent. I talked to friends who were stuck in the subway and gave them the incomprehensible news. Something we thought was permanent, proved to us that it wasn't. We would never see the desks in our office again – not the mugs, vases, family photos or stash of shoes to match our business suits. We would never attend a concert in the outdoor atrium, buy Broadway tickets at half-price in the lobby, or shop in our favorite stores in the underground mall – Coach, Gap or Nine West. Miraculously, everyone in my lucky thirteenth floor office survived.

I lost two friends – a former co-worker who was the friendliest guy I'd ever met, and a girl from a networking group who had been chatting with me a few weeks before about moving into her first apartment. They were both so young.

If I was grown-up before, 9/11 peeled off the last bit of my innocence. I used to feel like I had all the time in the world. Youth is deceptive in that way. I worked in the most iconic buildings in the U.S., perhaps even the world. As building tenants we could visit the observation deck for free, but I never did. I had been to the famous Windows on the World restaurant on the 107th floor for drinks or parties many times. I was sure one day I'd go to the 110th floor observation deck. It never occurred to me that I could lose that opportunity.

My grandmother used to say, "The young may die, but the old must die." All of life is impermanent, especially people. A tree or building may live hundreds, even thousands of years, but we don't have as much time. Average life expectancy for a Black woman in the United States is 78.5 years old, according to the Centers for Disease Control.[1] That's the age my mother was when she lost her life to breast cancer. That's an age my oldest sister will never reach, having lost her life to sickle-cell disease at only thirty-one.

We must spend our time wisely and be prepared for change when it comes.

After a few more years at the telecom, I took a job at an art college in Brooklyn. I wanted to work closer to home, but I also wanted to run from some of the corporate madness I had experienced. They were systematically firing all the Black people in my position. It's a long story for another book, but the writing was on the wall. I had to leave. As I write some of this, I realize I had told myself stories to the point I forgot they're not true. I couldn't go on a job interview and say I left my employer because of institutional racism that had me creeping toward a nervous breakdown. I couldn't tell them that I took a month off on a mental health leave of absence and looked for a new job at the advice of my therapist. Instead, I told them I wanted to work closer to home for the benefit of my young daughter. It was true, but with glaring omissions. My experiences are part of the many ways Black folks suffer, especially women. It's not just the micro and macro aggressions against us, it's the fact that we are not allowed to live authentically. If we talk about racism or sexism we're deemed angry, delusional, or labeled a bitch. Meanwhile, most of us, at least the ones who dare to operate outside arenas deemed appropriate by white society, go through life navigating a field of those land mines.

I worked at the college for less than a year before realizing it was just as awful as corporate America. My co-workers were faking grant documents the same way folks were faking sales contracts at my former employer. The art scene lifted my spirit, but the bureaucracy wasn't for me. Always able to make lemonade out of lemons, I squeezed an amazing photography class out of my time there. I surprised myself by falling in love with the quiet of the dark room. I realize now it was my first taste of silent retreat and meditation. I had gotten my MBA for free from the telecom company before they threw me (and us) away. I got most of my bachelor's degree paid for by another employer. I thought I was smart and had things figured out, but corporate America was full of surprises.

I decided it was time to own my own business. I always had an entrepreneurial spirit, trying just about every multi-level marketing business over the years from Amway to Mary Kay. I thought a franchise would be safer than creating my own start-up, just like I thought working for large corporations would be safer than working for small ones. I was in for an unpleasant surprise.

In 2006, after a little over two years in business, I realized the women's fitness franchise that I owned was coming undone. I clawed at it, prayed over it, sunk my entire heart and every nickel I had into it. I was deep into my Christian faith at that time, and I believed God had put me on a path to spread physical and spiritual healing. My ladies worked up a sweat and many met with me weekly for bible study in the beautiful green and purple office I had designed myself in the Brooklyn community that I loved. I read *The Purpose-Driven Life* by Rick Warren more than once. I prayed and read my bible every night, often crying. I was in church every Sunday listening to my amazing pastor share her beautiful and inspirational sermons.

It had been a few years since I walked away from my marriage. I wanted to be loved by a kind and faithful man. I wanted to continue to live in the house that I adored. I wanted to be able to support myself and my daughter and do work that I thought was important. I thought I was doing everything God required of me. I was doing His work. I begged God to send me someone to love me, to let me stay in my home and raise my daughter. She was only five, and my most recent relationship had already unraveled with a cruel betrayal.

The bills had piled so high I started receiving foreclosure notices. I had a mortgage on top of my mortgage. I wondered if I could turn my basement into another apartment – I was running out of options. Finally, like a cat pulled out of a tall oak tree against its will, clawing and scratching the whole way down, I dismantled everything. I notified the few employees I had left. I wrote a letter to my customers. I refunded money that I didn't really have. I sold my house. I moved into a small apartment with my now six-year-old daughter so she could finish out her school year. We moved to Atlanta in August. I was so traumatized; I couldn't talk about it for years without crying. My entire savings had turned to smoke. I was part of a lawsuit against the franchise company for overselling territories, but the case ended without even enough of an award to cover attorney's fees. It was a kick in the gut.

American culture had sold me a fairytale. Fall in love. Get married. Buy a big house. Have some kids. Take family vacations. Get a dog. Buy more stuff. Live happily ever after and when you die go straight to Christian heaven. In the United States, 23% of women aged 40-59 are on anti-depressants.[2] Over 14 million adults have an alcohol use disorder, and 10% have a drug use problem at some point in their lives.[3,4] Apparently the dream isn't working quite as planned. I know mine didn't.

In my personal life and through my twelve years working as a financial advisor after I moved to Atlanta, one thing I've learned is that money and stuff don't provide happiness even a little bit. I'll never forget working with a client who made over a million dollars per year. No matter what I said she didn't feel financially secure.

If we want to be genuinely happy,
we must loosen our mental and physical grip
on people, things and situations.

I spent decades grasping for a life that I thought I was supposed to live – not having it saddened me, but chasing it was worse. It reminds me of the zombies from *The Walking Dead* – always hungry, never nourished. I wanted the illusion of certainty that the American Dream offered, not realizing two things:

1) The American Dream was never created with Black people in mind.
2) There is no such thing as certainty, and if there were, life would be incredibly boring.

There is a saying, "People make plans and God laughs." Yes, God always has the last laugh by taking our lives in directions we never could have planned.

When you let go of the attachment to safety and certainty you can have your first glimpse of freedom.

Our attachment can show up in many ways – a house, job, family, or closet full of shoes – the possibilities are endless. No matter what you find yourself attached to, it will always be a source of pain, because nothing stays the same and nobody lives forever. The only constant we can count on is change – whether it's slow like the story of the frog in a pot of cold water who doesn't realize the temperature has reached boiling until it's too late, or quick like the unprecedented crash of the Twin Towers on 9/11.

We are not only attached to the roles things play in our lives, but the roles we expect people to play. I've noticed this type of attachment as a parent. My nineteen-year-old daughter thanks me frequently for allowing her to grow up and providing a safe place for her self-expression. In my experience, many parents are horrified when their children grow up and do adult things. When my daughter turned thirteen, one of her friends told me how sad she was on her own thirteenth birthday because adults didn't really like teenagers. That was a wake-up call for me. She was right. I was terrified as my daughter approached her first birthday as a teenager. That conversation with a child helped me embrace my daughter's teen years in a way that I wouldn't have otherwise.

It was a teachable moment that flowed from my daughter's friend to me, instead of the other way around. Children have a lot to teach us if we are willing to listen. It shifted my perspective on my daughter's coming of age and helped me release my attachment to her innocence so she could grow up with confidence and joy. Many parents don't have the good fortune of a lesson like that and refuse to let their kids leave the nest mentally or physically.

Our children will grow up whether we allow them to or not. Some parents remain in denial, and instead of providing a tender ear for a child making their own scary journey into adulthood, they alienate the very person they love the most by pressuring them to stay the same.

We can attach ourselves to both psychological elements and physical things. I've had family members who were hoarders and have often wondered what makes people hold on to yellowed newspapers, frayed sweaters, paperback books and other things long past their usefulness. I've watched *Hoarders* on television cautiously, between splayed fingers.

Attachment is the same, whether we cling to our memories or physical items from our past.

Change can be frightening, whether it's relinquishing old traditions, getting rid of frenemies or throwing out the blanket you used to cuddle with as a child. We transfer emotions to objects that have no way of reciprocating or absorbing our energy. We hold tight to things and get upset when someone disrupts our stuff. At the end of our lives we can't take anything with us – we might be buried in beautiful clothes and gold rings, but they will remain in the ground, while our spirit travels to its next destination. Even if you don't believe your spirit will survive your physical death, you know you must still leave your possessions behind.

As Notorious B.I.G. famously sung on his posthumous album, *Life After Death*, "Mo money, mo problems." And for most of us, more money means more stuff. How can we expect to grow, transform, or change into a better version of ourselves if we're unwilling to let go of the things that hold us back?

We cling to things that weigh us down, while people in need go without.

My heart moans when I think about the disparities in this world – many of us pack our garages to the brim, and folks in poorer nations may reuse a single pot for an entire family. It's as if a universal law is being violated. The irony is that the family sharing the single pot has the potential to be happier than the family in the mansion with the four-car garage overflowing with conspicuous consumption. If you haven't seen the movie *Happy* on Netflix, I highly recommend. It makes a great case for this assertion.

Releasing attachment to traditions, ideas and things that hold you back is one of the most beautiful gifts you can give yourself. As Erykah Badu famously sings in the song, "Bag Lady," which inspired the title of this drop, "You can't hurry up cuz you've got too much stuff."

Donate, recycle, discard, and create space, both mental and physical.

Marie Kondo has become famous by helping others release stuff. How ironic that many of the things we thought would make us happy are ultimately holding us back. One of Marie's rules is that you shouldn't keep anything in your home that doesn't "spark joy." Such a lovely ideal. Should that only be limited to things, or perhaps also cover questionable "friendships?" When the phone rings and you stare at it with dread, it's likely this person isn't bringing you joy.

This is not to encourage you to get rid of things that you need, but rather to recognize the difference between healthy needs and unhealthy attachments. Get rid of the clothes you haven't worn, the books you haven't read, the dishes you haven't used. Consider downsizing your home. Make room for something new. Pack light.

Sometimes people get confused thinking being "detached" means we don't love our children, families or friends. The reverse is true. Practicing non-attachment will help you make the most out of all your relationships. You will recognize more deeply how precious your time and relationships are, knowing that they won't last forever. You can build stronger bonds by being unafraid to have difficult conversations because you understand there will be a day when you must separate. You can strengthen your spirit by preparing for a time when things will be different. You realistically examine physical objects in your life for what they really are, without ascribing more meaning to them than they deserve. You can fully immerse yourself in moments of joy and pleasure without worrying about when they will end.

Detachment helps you recognize the value of every moment, stay present and develop flexibility.

I was struck when I read *Of Mice and Men* by John Steinbeck as a child. I don't remember much about the story, but I remember one character kept a little mouse in his pocket as a pet. He loved the mouse and squeezed it so tight he killed it. Then he got another mouse. Throughout the story this happened repeatedly. Until we learn to let go, we repeat this in our own lives. Grabbing on to things so tightly we hurt them and us. You've probably heard the saying, "If you love someone set them free."

We all instinctively desire freedom.
Slavery or servitude is the ultimate nightmare.
Yet through our fear, we grip the people,
traditions, and possessions in our lives so tightly
that we create pain for ourselves and our loved ones.

Attachment. Fear of change. Illusion of certainty. Oppressive traditions. They're all bags. I love the Harriet Tubman quote at the beginning of this drop. The first time I saw it, I thought it was about freedom and courage, and it is. What I realize now is there is no freedom when we are attached, and there is no courage when we're fearing change and clawing for certainty. Attachment keeps us in bondage. Let it go.

Affirmations for Detachment:
- ❖ I open my heart to new experiences and the joy of uncertainty.
- ❖ I understand the nature of everything in this world is temporary and that's okay.
- ❖ I release my attachments to things and people that don't spark joy in my life.
- ❖ If I desire a sense of permanence, I will seek refuge in my spiritual journey.

        (Repeat at least 2x per day.)

Reflection Questions:
- ❖ How do you feel when you look in your closets, pantry, bookshelves or Caller ID? What things or people are cluttering your life?
- ❖ What do you need to leave behind to move closer to your dreams?
- ❖ Are there ways you can show love to family and friends by loosening your grip?

Time to Get Still:
- ❖ Visit TrishAhjelRoberts.com/resources and access Meditation #7 for Detachment.

    (Try for at least 2x per week, but daily is ideal.)

Let's Pollinate!
- ❖ Take inventory of what brings you joy and what you can release.
- ❖ Set a SMART goal: Specific, Measurable, Attainable, emotionally Relevant and Timebound.
- ❖ Continue to work with your accountability partner.

Grooves for Fluttering:
- Erykah Badu. "Bag Lady." *Mama's Gun*, 2000.
- Mary J. Blige. "Baggage." *The Breakthrough*, 2005.
- Sting. "If You Love Somebody Set Them Free." *The Dream of the Blue Turtles*, 1985.
- Aleem. "Release Yourself." NIA Records, 1984.

Think-Through Films:
- *Happy.* Directed by Roko Belic. Wadi Rum Productions, 2011.
- *Minimalism: A Documentary About the Important Things.* Directed by Matt D'Avelia. Catalyst Films, 2016
- *The True Cost.* Directed by Andrew Morgan. Untold Creative, 2015.

Additional Resources:
- TrishAhjelRoberts.com/resources is your main portal for all resources.
- *Tidying Up* by Marie Kondo
- *The Purpose-Driven Life* by Rick Warren
- Notorious B.I.G. "Mo Money Mo Problems." *Life After Death,* 1997.
- Amazon, Audible, Google, YouTube and your local library

Eighth Drop: Lay Your Weapons Down

"When I let go of what I am,
I become what I might be."
- Lao Tzu

_____
_____
_____
_____

You've come a long way. I hope you see that. If you've been following along with each drop of nectar, you've taken time to heal, to connect, to develop spiritually and to identify your talents by developing self-awareness and authenticity. You've released a boatload of anger and now you're so damn lovely to be around, even you want to spend more time with YOU. You've freed yourself from attachment to things and ideas, and even people, but only in a good way. You've expanded your generous nature and are ready to shine your light. Now it's time to ask the Universe for help and let go of the need to control every damn thing. Lay your weapons down. It's time to surrender.

There was a time when I didn't believe in anything bigger than myself. The god concept that I was raised with never rang true for me. It wasn't until my husband cheated on me in our first year of marriage that I had to put my bags completely down and gaze my eyes toward the sky. There *had* to be something bigger than me. I couldn't deal with this world of heartbreak on my own. In this way, I willed God into existence for me. This was the beginning of my spiritual journey. I started with Joel Osteen and what I call "begging prayers," sounding like Spike Lee in *She's Gotta Have It*. I used to pray and cry, begging God to let me keep my house or send someone to love me. I clung to what I knew with hands gripped so tight I couldn't open them to receive my rightful blessings. It reminds me of when I learned to swim; I first had to learn to float – to make peace with the water. If I fought it, I could drown. In my life, I had been thrashing. I was trying to control a world so complex even leading scientists and spiritual practitioners can't understand it. Even if it were only my little world – my job, home, relationship, I still couldn't control it. I was drowning.

In the Christian faith we say, "Let go and let God." In Buddhism we embrace the wisdom of each moment. In yogic philosophy we bring our awareness to the present. I would imagine other religions and ancient teachings have similar lessons of surrender. As we practice the sweetness of letting go, we must also ask the Universe for help. We should absolutely let go, but we also need to let our intentions be known. Have you ever had a friendship or relationship with someone who thought you were a mind-reader? Perhaps they were angry and wouldn't tell you why. Don't be that person in your relationship with the world.

If the Universe doesn't know what you want,
it stands to reason that neither do you.
If it hasn't been articulated,
more likely than not, it hasn't been defined
in your own mind.

So how do we create and share our desires with the Universe? How do we make ourselves the squeaky wheel so when all the gods and goddesses get together for tea, we come up in conversation?

We are creating a powerful foundation by setting our intentions, following the guided meditations and repeating affirmations. Listening to music that reinforces your goals through the playlists I've created also shows intention and raises your vibration. I grew up in the '70s and '80s and the Beach Boys had a song called "Good Vibrations." While it's not in my playlist now, it was a big hit. Back then I thought vibrations were some hippie thing from California. In the '90s I thought vibes were the feeling I got from being with a great group of people. Since then, I've learned that humans do operate on various frequencies, and your level of consciousness can literally raise or lower that vibration.

It's commonly understood that the human brain operates in one of five waveforms: Gamma, Beta, Alpha, Theta and Delta. Gamma is an alert state for problem solving and concentration. Beta is a busy and active mind. Alpha is a restful and reflective mind. Theta is drowsiness. Finally, Delta is the sleep or dream state.[1] When I studied yoga nidra, I learned there are seven stages of consciousness recognized by yogis, each aligning with these brain rhythms.[2] When we learn to meditate or practice yoga nidra, we can expand our usual level of awareness.

Music also has a profound effect on our brain waves.[3] Sound bathing with Tibetan bowls is an excellent example. The first time I experienced a sound bath, I was shocked by how deeply relaxed I felt afterward. I was familiar with the euphoria of meditation but adding the reverberation of the bowls took my experience over the top. If you haven't experienced a sound bath, I highly encourage you to explore. You can find this type of music on all the major music streaming platforms.

These practices of consciously or unconsciously engaging our brain waves changes the signals we emit to others. You may have heard the word aura used to reference the electromagnetic energy field that surrounds each of us. When we meet people for the first time we take in their physical appearance, posture and energy (aura). That's why 55% of communication is considered body language, while 38% is tone of voice, leaving only 7% for the actual words.[4] We speak volumes before we open our mouths.

I led a workshop at the beginning of 2020 on electronic vision-boarding. Every time I sit down at my laptop, a beautiful display of my intentions reminds me of what I'm working toward. My current vision board is my third. I created the first one after watching the movie, *The Secret*. Honestly, I got it mostly wrong the first time. My vision board was full of things I thought I was supposed to want – cars, money, a relationship with a white guy. (I've posted them online so you can see what I'm talking about.) The things that I really wanted came to fruition - a healthier lifestyle with yoga, biking and nature. The rest of it didn't happen because I didn't really want those things.

By the time I created my second vision board I had a better sense of myself. I had already fallen in love with Modern Buddhism, then I attended a yoga retreat weekend and learned about goddesses. The retreat rekindled my love for African and Greek storytelling from my elementary and high school days. (I was fortunate to have had an African storyteller regularly visit my elementary school class. I still remember sitting in a circle and listening to Anansi the Spider and Aesop's fables with childhood delight.) The yoga instructor must have awakened my inner goddess, because from then I decided I *was* a goddess – my self-love was ripening, and I began seeing myself in a new way. Of course, a beautiful Buddha and goddess would be on my vision board!

The central image was a Buddha statue taken from the May 2006 cover of *Shambhala Sun* magazine, now called *Lion's Roar*. She looked like she was ready to take on the world. I later learned she was Kuan Yin (female Buddha of compassion). I paired her with Aphrodite (goddess of love) and surrounded them with yoga, travel, writing and philanthropy. This second vision board was much more effective and honest. I still enjoy looking at it from time to time to see how far I've come.

If you decide to build a vision board, make sure it's a real stretch. I say that because vision-boarding has become a bit of a trend to the point that it seems to have lost meaning in some arenas. I remember meeting someone who told me she had five vision boards, and I've met people who say they make a new one every year. That's not a vision board, that's a craft project.

A vision board should last at least a few years before you feel like you've made enough progress to change it.

It doesn't mean you can't update your board every year – that may even be a good thing. But, if you're trashing your board every year and starting over, you didn't spend enough time on it with the first go-round. Handwriting additions onto your existing board or updating your e-vision board is okay – I just want your vision to be a real vision from your heart, without barriers. Imagine your life completely self-actualized, satisfying your wildest dreams, and leaving your best legacy. If you do it right, your vision board will scare you a little bit. Don't worry if it's not perfect the first time. Mine wasn't, and I still made a lot of progress toward my goals.

I remember when I posted the word "write" on my second vision board. It was plain and indistinct, but its presence on my board terrified me. I reluctantly rubbed my glue stick on the back of the magazine cut-out. Was I really going to do this? I stopped writing for twenty years after *Chocolate Soufflé*. It's incomprehensible to me now. Writing is my greatest love, but I had thrown in the towel long ago. Putting it on the board meant I had to confront my desires and my failures. *What if I failed again?* I wouldn't be able to pretend I didn't really want it anyway if it's sitting up on a damn board hanging on the wall in my bedroom.

I've learned that to be successful you have to be comfortable with failure. I've never been a person who cared much about what other people think of me. What goes on in your head about me or anything else is your own business. But still, putting myself out into the world as a writer terrified me. Now, it's my greatest joy.

Now when I pray to the Universe and all the holy beings, I ask to grow qualities in myself that will help others. I've come a long way from my "please baby, please baby, baby please" prayers. If you don't know what I'm talking about, you've got to watch *She's Gotta Have It*. The original 1986 film is streaming on Netflix with just about all of Spike Lee's creations.

If you keep expressing gratitude, setting intentions, meditating, saying affirmations and praying wisely positive change will manifest in your life.

I've had the opportunity to participate in burning ceremonies at the sweat lodge and at local yoga studios. This is another wonderful way to set intention. I particularly enjoy it as a New Year's ritual. Sometimes instead of just expressing what we want, we need to let the Universe know what we DO NOT want. You can do this at home, but be careful – burning the house down will not make your dreams come true. You simply write what you want to get rid of on a piece of paper and watch the paper burn while you concentrate on releasing. The easiest place to do this is in a fireplace, outdoor grill or barbecue pit, but you can also safely use a candle outdoors. It's important to *watch the paper burn* – it sends a powerful message to your subconscious mind. When I've participated in ceremonial burnings, I usually guard my paper so nobody can see the shit I'm dealing with, but I'm past that point with you, so here it is: I've burned fear many times. I've burned self-doubt, selfishness, excess and inconsistency. Whatever you need to release, write it down and watch it burn away and disappear from your life. When you're finished, take a few moments to reflect on the release you experienced.

You can achieve what you set your mind on and what you ask for. It can't be one without the other. If your dream is a secret to the Universe it can't come to fruition.

Protect your dream from dream-killers. There are going to be folks who can't stand that you even have a dream. They may become part of the pruning. I saw a meme recently: "You cannot talk Butterfly language with Caterpillar people." I don't know who wrote it, but I wish it were me. You can't elevate if you allow yourself to be surrounded with negativity. Depending on your surroundings, you may need to keep your dream quiet for now. It's a double-edged sword. If nobody knows your dream, they can't try to kill it; they also can't try to help you. Tread carefully. You might already have folks asking what you're doing with this book. Just smile and nod. The path you're on is not for everyone.

Aside from meditation, there are other stillness practices that can be phenomenal ways to let the Universe guide you. I attended a partially silent meditation retreat in 2015. I shared a cabin with two people, and we didn't talk until noon each day. It was remarkable how relaxing it was not having to think about what to say, especially around strangers. If it's practical, you can try this at home. Just stop talking for an hour or two. Notice if you're more relaxed.

You might also try a simple stillness practice. Don't worry about following a guided meditation, just sit in stillness. You can set the stage with soft lighting, incense, a candle or ambient music in the background if you'd like. You can search for yoga or ambient music on any of the music apps. If you don't have time for all of that, don't worry, just take a seat somewhere and be still for a few minutes – like a grown-up timeout.

There are other lovely ways to incorporate stillness practices into your life if you want to go deeper and be in community. You might want to look for yoga nidra, guided visualization or restorative yoga in your neighborhood and online. I will continue to add to my online and retreat offerings.

Be aware that sometimes stillness can bring out unexpected emotions. These are typically emotions that you normally ignore rising to the surface.

Remember, you are always in control.
You can open your eyes, move your body
or come out of a visualization
that makes you uncomfortable.

I can't even begin to express how incorporating stillness into my life has opened what feels like a direct portal to Divine intelligence. In those moments of quiet reflection, I realize I'm only partly responsible for what I've attained and experienced in this life. In that realization I've found clarity and humility.

Our experience in this world is not only us – it's much larger than we are. I attended a class where Deepak Chopra spoke about the internal biosphere of our bodies and the external biosphere which consists of everything else. His talk mirrored a poem I wrote while in yoga teacher training in 2019. I enjoy sharing poems, mantras and affirmations when I teach. This one speaks to our unity with nature, and reading it still brings me a gentle feeling of peace:

You are as much a bee
As a bee.
You are as much a blossom
As a blossom.
You are as much the ocean
As the ocean.

You are the drop in the ocean, and you *are* the ocean. If we didn't know we were connected globally through a single biosphere, COVID-19 corrected us. We are one with the world. What happens to one of us affects all of us. As you grow and transform, you will elevate your environment, just like a rose planted in your window box elevates your home.

I know we are all starting from different places. Just know that no matter how difficult things may be right now, what's on the other side is absolutely beautiful.

Don't give up. Don't fight it. Accept it, be still, respect it, and surrender.

Affirmations for Surrender:

(Write your own affirmations asking for what you want.)

- I am a _____. (Say it as if it already happened for you.)
- I want to be a _____. (Dream even bigger.)
- My greatest heart's desire is to _____.
  (Make the dream so big it scares you.)

  (Repeat at least 2x per day.)

Reflection Questions:

- What do you enjoy doing so much that you completely lose track of time? How can you include these activities in your vision?
- What do you want people to remember about you when you are no longer on this earth?
- What can you do to let God and/or the Universe know your intentions?

Time to Get Still:

- Choose your own stillness practice this week, or visit TrishAhjelRoberts.com/resources and access Meditation #8 for Surrender.

  (Enjoy at least 2x per week, but daily is ideal.)

Let's Pollinate!

- Make a commitment to identify your vision for your life and ask the Universe for help. Consider creating a vision board, either paper or electronic.
- Set a SMART goal: Specific, Measurable, Attainable, emotionally Relevant and Timebound.
- Continue to work with your accountability partner.

Grooves for Fluttering:
- Whitney Houston. "Exhale (Shoop Shoop)." *Waiting to Exhale*, 1995.
- Sly and The Family Stone. "Que Será, Será (Whatever Will Be, Will Be)." *Fresh*, 1973.
- Lee Ann Womack. "I Hope You Dance." *I Hope You Dance*, 2000.
- Bob Marley and the Wailers. "Three Little Birds." *Exodus*, 1977.

Think-Through Films:
- *She's Gotta Have It*. Directed by Spike Lee. Starring Tracy Camilla Johns. 40 Acres & A Mule Filmworks, 1986.
- *Eat, Pray, Love*. Directed by Ryan Murphy. Starring Julia Roberts. Columbia Pictures, 2010.
- *The Secret*. Directed by Drew Heriot. Documentary. Prime Time Productions, 2006.

Additional Resources:
- TrishAhjelRoberts.com/resources is your main portal for all resources.
- Chitrasukhu.com
- Traceeyoga.com
- Amazon, Audible, Google, YouTube and your local library

Ninth Drop: Patience is the Truth

"Rome wasn't built in a day."
- Proverbs

I hope you feel your progression on this beautiful journey we've embarked on. I feel it deep in my soul as I write for you. You've been presented with a lot of ideas, and I hope you are beginning to feel an internal shift. A movement toward healing, self-awareness, self-love, community, generosity, freedom, focused intention and the sweet release of surrender. We surrender to what is. We surrender to what we don't know. Most importantly, we surrender to time.

When I was a teenager, I wrote a long poem about my lack of desire or interest in patience. I knew it was supposed to be a virtue, but I didn't care. I wanted what I wanted, and I wanted it *now*. Since then, I've realized that overnight sensations can be decades in the making. Anything worth having is worth waiting for. And working for. And, it's a lot more fun when you enjoy the process.

At times, I've wanted things so desperately without having the wisdom to know what was best. I've wanted the wrong men and the wrong jobs, and I was unhappy when I got them.

I've wanted houses, cars and businesses without fully understanding the responsibility of ownership. I've longed for a husband and hungered for divorce. I've learned I'm not alone. I've wanted things I've never experienced, and then, when I got them, I didn't want them anymore.

We may be young and high on hormones with a strong desire for a motorcycle without the wisdom to handle the speed. Or, we may want a spouse before we are ready for monogamy, vulnerability or compromise. We may want a high-powered job at the same time we long to become a parent, without an understanding that both endeavors require hands-on time and we only have twenty-four hours in a day.

> **We can't see into the future,
> and we don't always know what's best for us.
> Delays give us a chance to prepare
> for whatever's coming our way.**

For most of us, when we have a dream that hasn't yet come to fruition, we want it now. We can't wait, and any waiting that is forced upon us feels cruel. The uncertainty of the future seems unkind, yet we might be completely unprepared for the reality of the dream. You've probably heard the story of lotto recipients who blow through their winnings in a short period of time. I worked in retail banking for seven years as a financial advisor and had the opportunity to work with more than one lottery winner. I can confirm the statistics. There have been countless stories of young celebrities who, unprepared for the demands of fame, lost their lives to drugs, loneliness and depression. Billie Holiday. Jimi Hendrix. Marvin Gaye. Whitney Houston.

The New Oxford American Dictionary defines patience as "the capacity to accept or tolerate delay, trouble or suffering without getting angry or upset." In my youth I thought patience meant that I *liked* waiting for what I wanted *now*. I was never going to like that. However, by not accepting the waiting I was making myself anxious and unhappy. I was missing out on enjoying my life. We may never get what we want. When we lack patience, we waste time anxiously waiting for something that may never arrive. By gracefully accepting reality, we open the door for truth and wisdom.

Patience allows us to endure an uncomfortable situation with tolerance, even bliss. When I surrendered to the sweetness of life and stopped pushing for all my perceived goals, my impatience turned to joy. Once I realized my time must subjugate itself to Divine time, I could relax and just be. I believe that's the essence of patience, and it's indescribably peaceful.

In this way, I see patience as a form of mindfulness. In Kadampa Buddhism we often talk of "patient acceptance" in every moment. Each moment is what it is, and it's exactly as it's supposed to be. There's no point in worrying about the next moment or past moments. The only time we have any control over is the moment that we're in. The only decision to make is what we're doing right now. When the moment feels good, we don't need a strategy.

Patience is accepting moments that don't feel good. These unloved moments are still the truth, whether we like them or not.

You may have heard people say they're taking it "one day at a time" when dealing with drug, alcohol, or even food addiction. The reality is they are taking it "moment by moment." The decision to say no to harmful substances or undesirable behaviors happens in the confines of a second. Each decision can get you through to the next moment. These split seconds daisy chain into a better life. We all know people who have struggled with addictive behaviors without the additional stress and lack of privacy that stems from celebrity.

This is not to say everyone with a big dream wants to be a celebrity, however the word itself means "celebrated." So, if you want to be the best singer, writer, speaker, chef, businessperson or scientist, you may accidentally find yourself being so celebrated that you're under someone else's microscope. I've heard conversations where people say actors and singers "knew what they signed up for." Perhaps some did, but I'm sure many were just driven to pursue their art.

Getting too much of anything too soon is more of a curse than gift.

For the uninitiated, success and fame don't sound like something to worry about – lots of money, sex, travel and prestige at first glance sounds like a great time. However, if you're a bit more thoughtful, success may mean a lot of people are depending on you for their incomes. You may not be able to cancel a commitment so easily anymore. If you drink a few too many at a party, it may end up on TMZ for the world to judge. You may not be able to go to the pharmacy to buy Monistat as Gabrielle Union relayed hilariously in her book, *We're Going to Need More Wine*. People may want to know personal details of your heartache and pain when you are still trying to process them yourself. You may completely lose your privacy to the point where you a need a private jet to fly you to a remote island in order to take a vacation. No more Disney World.

These are dramatic examples, but the fear of success is real, and it's not without good reason. Many times, we don't know what prevents us from moving forward. Sometimes our subconscious holds us back because we are not ready.

Without a solid foundation, dreams coming true can lead to disaster. This book is helping you lay that solid foundation, so when the time is right you are more than ready for whatever your heart desires.

As a child I was taught patience is a virtue, as an adult I've come to understand that patience is a learned skill that comes from mindfully accepting each moment as it arises without anger. It allows me to steep in my emotions and infuses me with unfiltered truth. Instead of trying to dictate what the moment should be, I have learned to flow with it.

When the world doesn't move at my preferred pace, I look for messages in the detours.

When I'm in traffic, I give thanks that I'm not the reason for the traffic. I wonder if the delay is keeping me safe in a way that I don't understand. In my mind, I wish other travelers happiness and a safe journey. When a business endeavor doesn't happen according to my schedule, I look for the lessons. What did I learn by doing the work? Did a missed attempt reroute me to a better place?

In the summer of 2019, I began planning a large retreat at Callaway Gardens, a beautiful resort about an hour south of Atlanta. When I realized it was also home to a butterfly sanctuary, I decided it was meant to be! I put together a team of amazing presenters and began promoting the event. I wanted it to be large and inclusive, unlike previous events that I had done for my Black Vegan Life™ group that were more intimate. As I continued to promote the event, I knew something wasn't right.

I remember tossing and turning in my bed when I went to visit my ailing father in Brooklyn four months before the scheduled date of the event. I was coming up on the deadline for my final headcount and I didn't have enough people. I didn't know if it was the wrong messaging or the wrong timing. I knew my content was phenomenal. With bittersweet surrender, I pulled the plug on the event long before the coronavirus pandemic pulled it for me. It wasn't what I wanted, but I've learned to flow with my life. Clearly there was something around the corner – I just couldn't see it yet. I didn't worry about the money I had spent. At minimum, I knew I had learned a lot, established new relationships and refined my personal mission.

The retreat was called "Thinking Outside the Chrysalis." It gave birth to the idea for this book. I was sleeping one night, my thoughts full of ideas for the retreat, sending my daughter off to college, quitting my job and selling my house. Even with my experience as a meditation instructor, my mind was busy. I often find my best ideas bubble to the surface in the stillness of meditation, sleep or restorative yoga. I woke up in the middle of the night and jotted down the titles for ten chapters that would later morph into the twelve "drops" presented here. It was conceived as a book that would be delivered to retreat participants, but the Universe had its own plans.

I call this practice of seeking out silver linings, "Beauty in the Detours," and wrote about it in my February 5, 2020 blog. This book will reach many more people than my retreat ever could. Had I pushed forward with the retreat, it would have been displaced by the looming quarantine.

The 2020 pandemic was a detour we all had to suffer. It's given us a global opportunity to look for the beauty. It's also given the world an opportunity to work on our patience.

Because of the new popularity of virtual offerings, I will host my first virtual retreat. I love meeting people in person, but there are benefits to meeting online: you can interact with people from all over the country and the world at a low cost; you don't have to travel; and, if you have a quiet, private space in your home, you can be as goofy as you want to be. I attended a Chopra retreat where we were taught self-massage. By the time I was finished I was half-naked and slathered in my favorite oil. I couldn't have done that in a room full of strangers.

I was supposed to attend a yoga teacher training in Ghana in March 2020, right before Ghana closed its borders. I hope that through my virtual offerings I might meet my African cohorts online before I ever meet them in person.

Life is full of uncertainty.
It's in this place of ambiguity where we find infinite potential.
Patience allows it to unfold without restriction.
Our job is to open our eyes so we can see it.

When we accept the moments that arise instead of trying to deny them, we can find the message. Maybe the purpose of waiting in line, waiting for social media followers, getting sick, or getting passed over for a promotion is to slow you down. Stop, take a breath, and notice if you can find the beauty. Make some time for stillness and see if the lesson arises. There is always a lesson.

We can get so busy, the entire Universe is screaming to slow down, and we're too distracted to listen.

When a relationship doesn't happen as I would have liked, I wonder, is it because I'm not ready to connect with the right person yet? Don't get me wrong, it's very easy for women to connect with the *wrong* person. Potential partners are everywhere. My question is: Do I still have emotional and spiritual work to do before I can even identify another kindred soul – a person who can be a committed friend and a lover? I'd rather be joyfully alone, rejoicing in my freedom, than suffering in the confines of a bad relationship.

I've been married twice. My first marriage was suggested by my parents because I was only eighteen, and I wanted to live with my boyfriend. My parents didn't want me to live "in sin." This was 1987 when that was still a thing. He was physically abusive. We only lived together for nine months. I rushed in and I ran out.

The second time I married was ten years later. Now I was twenty-eight and itching for the American Dream I've referenced throughout this book. I rushed because I already felt the tick of my biological clock. I had my daughter at thirty-two, and instead of glowing in gratitude, I was disappointed that I didn't have her earlier, according to my arbitrary schedule.

There's a quote I love from the movie, *Thelma and Louise*. Susan Sarandon's character says to her husband, "We both got what we settled for." So true and profound. I've decided I will only settle for the highest levels of joy and fulfillment in my life. I will not allow anyone to rain on my parade.

Now that I realize the Universe speaks in ways that are not particularly comfortable, it's easier for me to be patient. Now that I understand the Universe is working on my behalf, I don't have to push for everything. Now when I'm in traffic I listen to a podcast, audiobook, my *Thinking Outside the Chrysalis* playlist, or other music I enjoy. When I'm in line I look for a good article to read, take deep breaths or do a short meditation. When a business venture doesn't work out, I look for ways to hone my skills and connections for the next opportunity.

We can't control the output.
We can only control the input.
Choose to give your passion, focus and energy to the world and confidently, joyfully and patiently wait for what is to manifest.

Affirmations for Patience:
- When I have to wait, I use my time wisely and joyfully.
- When I wait, I have an opportunity to unlock the power of stillness.
- When things don't unfold as I would like, I look for the lessons.

   (Repeat at least 2x per day.)

Reflection Questions:
- Have you noticed a time in your life when lack of patience made you unhappy?
- Can you think of positive ways to spend your time while you wait?
- Are you working toward a goal that requires your patience?

Time to Get Still:
- Choose your own stillness practice this week, or visit TrishAhjelRoberts.com/resources and access Meditation #9 for Patience.

   (Enjoy at least 2x per week, but daily is ideal.)

Let's Pollinate!
- Make a commitment to notice when you are being impatient and if you can use your time in a more beneficial way.
- Set a SMART goal: Specific, Measurable, Attainable, emotionally Relevant and Timebound.
- Continue to work with your accountability partner.

Grooves for Fluttering:
- India Arie. "Slow Down" *Voyage to India*, 2002.
- Otis Redding. "(Sittin' On) the Dock of the Bay." *The Dock of the Bay*, 1968.
- Bob Marley and the Wailers. "Easy Skanking" *Kaya*, 1978.
- The Beatles. "Let It Be" *Let It Be*, 1970.

Think-Through Films:

- *The Pursuit of Happyness.* Directed by Gabriele Muccino. Starring Will Smith and Jaden Smith. Columbia Pictures, 2006.
- *The Prophet.* Directed by Roger Allers. Starring Liam Neeson and Salma Hayek. Ventanarosa, 2014.
- *Thelma and Louise.* Directed by Ridley Scott. Starring Susan Sarandon and Geena Davis. Pathé Entertainment, 1991.

Additional Resources:

- TrishAhjelRoberts.com/resources is your main portal for all resources.
- Kadampa.org
- Chopra.com
- Amazon, Audible, Google, YouTube and your local library

Tenth Drop: Don't Eat the Dead

"The living shouldn't eat the dead."
- Unknown

_____
_____
_____
_____

Can you believe we've made it to drop ten?! I know you're making amazing progress in hitting that next level of sweetness in your life. Now for the kicker: if you want to experience true happiness in this world you can't benefit from the misfortune, oppression and abuse of others. It seems pretty obvious at first glance, but when we delve deeper, elevating our level of compassion can be the trickiest drop of all.

Treating others the way we would like to be treated is the foundation of compassion, and the basis for both Christianity and Buddhism. If you were raised Christian like most people in the Western hemisphere you know the main philosophy of Jesus Christ is "Do unto others as you would have them do unto you." You've also heard, "What you have done to the least of my brothers, so you have done to me," and "Love thy neighbor."[1] For Buddhists, the concept of compassion is so foundational, even insects are protected from harm.

In our modern world those sayings aren't much more than meaningless platitudes. At best, they're the source of an internal struggle against what we believe to be our selfish nature. Perhaps we make an effort to be kind, to donate to the needy or to bake an extra batch of cookies for our neighbor. But, when we look around, it seems many people have done well in this world by stealing, cheating, lying and killing. Our history is full of colonizers and the businesses they created through slavery and genocide. Since you're reading this book, I believe you want more than that brutal heritage and legacy. Scamming may get you money and power, but it will never get you the joy and peace that comes from clarity of consciousness. Harming others may tease you with a glimpse of antagonistic glee but can never bring true joy or fulfillment. This explains why so many wealthy people drown in their own loneliness and misery. If you don't believe it, read about Leona Helmsley and the millions she left to her dog.[2]

A person without a conscience is deemed a sociopath. For the rest of us regular folks, doing things that hurt others gives us a sense of malaise whether large or small, conscious or unconscious. When I was in college, I learned the term "cognitive dissonance." *Psychology Today* defines it as "the state of discomfort felt when two or more modes of thought contradict each other." For me, it's the discomfort and anxiety I feel when my actions are not in line with my values. As a sexual assault survivor, I think I've made myself a little more educated about prostitution and pornography than most folks. The average age for a sex-trafficking victim to first have sex for money is between twelve and nineteen according to various sources. As the mother of a nineteen-year-old, both numbers are babies to me. I'm certainly no angel, but I avoid strip clubs and porn because I don't want to benefit from the exploitation of others. More than half of prostitutes are both victims of childhood sexual assault and physical violence.[3] I would expect similar numbers for other sex workers. When I was young, ignorance was bliss. As Maya Angelou famously said, "Do the best you can until you know better. Then when you know better, do better."

When I was in my early twenties, I had a friend who stripped at a night club in New Jersey. At the time, it was against state law to be topless. The girls wore bikini tops and thong bottoms. At the time, "stripping your way through college" was a popular theme in TV movies, and I considered it an option. I was tall and slim. Dancing in a bikini sounded like fun to my naïve mind. I went to the club, and my eyes opened to reality. I knew what fun looked like, and this wasn't it. The dressing room bustled as young girls and older women sniffed cocaine and threw back vodka shots – none of them would go on stage sober. I quickly realized why. Their bikinis were often pulled to the side to allow full display of their privates. Drunken men were loud and disrespectful. It was a job, but it wasn't a job anyone would want unless they were desperate.

I used to think stripping, prostitution and pornography were victimless crimes. Now I know the victim is on both sides of the transaction. Whether it's the johns who are desperate for gratification, connection, power or self-esteem, or it's the sex workers desperate for money to feed themselves, their families or their addictions. Stripping is certainly better than prostitution and pornography, but not much. Your spirit suffers when you engage in activities that go against your values, even if you don't know what your values are. When I talk about the spirit in my second drop, that sense of self is good, Divine and solid, even if your self-awareness hasn't risen to meet it yet. In yoga teacher training we were taught about two selves, the one we commonly refer to with the lowercase "s" and our Divine self, represented by an upper case "S." For Christians, you might think of this Self as the holy spirit or holy ghost. This part of you is always there, even if you're not familiar with it yet.

Sexism also plays a part. When young men and boys are desperate, they don't typically become strippers or sex workers. They may become drug dealers or stick-up kids. And, of course, racism plays a part, because people in distressed communities are often Black and Hispanic – everyone working with the hand they've been dealt.

The machine that powers institutional racism knows the power of self-exploitation. When you consume products that exploit others, through pornography, prostitution or strip clubs, you stunt your own happiness. The effect goes even further when the people you exploit look like your own family. Like your own mother. Like you.

We live in complex societies, designed to keep us disconnected from the products we consume, whether it's pornography or violence.

It took many years for me to make the connection between violence and the Standard American Diet. When I was growing up, the staples in our family refrigerator were milk, orange juice, cheese, eggs, bacon and bologna. In the pantry we always had sliced bread, cereal and crackers. I was lucky to have grown up with both of my parents and my grandmother, so there was a homecooked meal every evening – always a meat, vegetable and starch. The vegetables usually weren't very tasty, and I didn't care much for starches like rice or potatoes, so I filled up on the meat, whether it was chicken, fish, goat, steak, or, my favorite, oxtails. When I was eighteen and moved into my first apartment with my new husband, I remember cooking a burger in the microwave and placing it on toasted white bread for our first meal. Thinking about that makes me cringe when I realize how disconnected I was from the source of my food back then. I didn't know where my "hamburger meat" came from, nor did I understand the ingredients in my bread.

I never gave any thought to meat consumption until I was in graduate school in 1999. We did a case study on the meatpacking industry while I was working on my MBA. I learned that Jell-o comes from boiling scraps of skin, tendons, ligaments and bones. A few months later, I saw the controversial *Sensation* exhibit at the Brooklyn Museum, featuring thought-provoking and troubling depictions of farm animals cut apart and immersed in formaldehyde. It was the first time I saw the faces of the animals I ate.[4] After that, I decided to give up red meat. In 2008 I watched an episode of *The Oprah Winfrey Show* where she showed clips from the movie, *Food, Inc.* I finally began to wake up to the truth. I saw unnaturally large chickens trying to walk ankle-deep in feces in a dark, cavernous barn. They kept falling into piles of communal shit because their little legs couldn't support their enormous bodies. They would never see daylight. It was too horrifying to even understand. My mind immediately went to the Perdue oven-stuffer roasters my mom liked to buy. *Was this where they came from?*

After years of going back and forth between giving up red meat or chicken, I attended a compassion retreat at Kadampa Meditation Center in Atlanta in 2012 and finally committed to going vegetarian. I'm certainly not judge and jury on anything, but I know right from wrong even when I break my own rules. I know the first commandment is "Though shalt not kill," and I know the first tenet in yoga is "Ahimsa" or non-violence. I know Jesus gave us the golden rule, and I know Buddha said not to believe what anyone taught unless it made sense in my own heart. I stopped eating animals because once I awakened to the truth, I felt guilty when I sat down to eat. I felt like a hypocrite saving bugs, rescuing dogs and eating chicken. (And, yes, I used to foster dogs in my home.)

I stopped eating animals to save myself
– my heart, my joy and my freedom.

When I first moved to Atlanta, I used to take my daughter to a place called Yellow River Game Ranch. We would walk along dirt paths with our carrot sticks, apple slices, celery stalks and peanuts to feed the animals we encountered. There were metal dispensers along the trail that released a handful of food pellets for a quarter. Incredibly beautiful chickens would walk out in front of us. Gentle deer would eat right out of our hands.

As we approached the donkeys they would kick and bray, shaking the confines of the wooden fence around them. The ducks splashed in the pond and demanded food with their loud quacking.

Even though I had the unusual good fortune to have a summer home in the country as a child, I was disconnected from nature. To me, food came from the supermarket. I can only imagine how disconnected I would have been if I'd never had the opportunity to leave the city on a regular basis. My childhood summers were marked by the smell of honeysuckle, cut grass and rum and cokes. They sang the rhythm of birds, thunderstorms and calypso. But, I never saw donkeys and sheep turn up like at the Yellow River Game Ranch. It was different. It was wild. It felt really good interacting with animals in such an intimate way. Since then I've learned animal therapy is a real thing. Animals can provide many therapeutic benefits including decreased risk of depression, reduced anxiety and lower blood pressure and stroke risk.[5]

I come from a home where my parents indulged my three sisters and me with pets. I'm grateful to have grown up with dogs, cats and even a bird. They were imperfect relationships, but I value what each animal brought to my life whether it was companionship, a playmate or simply compassion. My favorite childhood dog was named Honey. She was a beautiful collie mix. I was about five years old and bumped my head on something. Honey came over and licked my boo-boo. In retrospect, I realize our pets were considered entertainment, more than anything else. If caring for them became too difficult, they had to go. One day I came home, and Honey was gone. I never found out what happened to her. My guess is she was given to another family or taken to a shelter. I was guilty of much of the same behavior when I became an adult. The apple doesn't fall far from the tree unless wise hands lift it higher. Eventually I learned that we are all animals sharing this earth together and deserve equal respect. My wise hands were education. Now I'm mom to a very spoiled, rescued puppy named Cooper. You can follow him on Instagram at vegan_cavachon.

When we don't respect all sentient beings and the living environment around us, we create unanticipated problems. Whether it's infectious diseases like COVID-19 or E. coli, lifestyle diseases like diabetes or heart disease, or the global climate crisis, every action creates a reaction.

In the movie, *We Are One*, there is a remarkable story about the extinction of the dodo bird in Mauritius, an island off the southeast coast of Africa. The bird was critical to the growth of the most important tree on the island, calvaria major, which was used to build ships. When dodos were hunted to the point of extinction, it was discovered that in order for the seeds to take root they had to pass through the digestive system of the dodo bird. Birds were imported from surrounding countries, but none could do the job. The tree then went extinct as well. The island was forced to change its primary production from wood to sugar cane. In doing so, it imported workers from India who ultimately overtook the reigning culture. So, from the loss of a single species of bird, the people of Mauritius lost their language and their culture. While there is debate about the details of this theory, there is no question that we are all connected.

We cannot harm others, intentionally or innocently, and walk away unscathed. This is part of Universal law and justice. Just as in the laws created by people, gross negligence is a crime, and ignorance is not a defense.

Some may refer to the effect as Karma. You simply can't harm others and walk away unaffected. If you want to be a nudist or have three husbands, go for it. The problem begins when your choices harm others. So if your three husbands are actually someone else's husbands, that's a problem. If you're driving down the highway nude, that's an issue. And, if you're buying packaged meats, then you can't convince yourself you're not harming anyone, because you're actually eating someone.

Most people in the U.S. cannot imagine eating a dog because it's considered unspeakable here. However, most Americans don't realize experiments are conducted on dogs in laboratories every day. According to peta.org more than 65,000 dogs are tormented in U.S. laboratories daily, with beagles being the favorite breed because they are considered particularly sweet and docile. The Beagle Freedom Project is a non-profit that works specifically to rehome beagles that have been used in experiments.

Despite everything I learned along the way it took me about ten years to finally stop eating animals, and even longer to awaken to other types of animal cruelty. Dogs aren't the only animals subject to cruel experimentation and mutilation. Chimpanzees, cats, guinea pigs, and rats are all used for experiments in the U.S.

The more I learned the more outraged I became. It was like opening Pandora's box. I noticed a move toward cage-free eggs in my local supermarket. I learned that wire cages are used to stack chickens one on top of the other, so that the chickens on top urinate and defecate on the chickens on the bottom. I later learned our African ancestors were stacked the same way on slave ships. Urine, feces and menses all flowing from the upper levels to the people below. It's unconscionable, yet it happened and it's still happening.

When I first went vegan and didn't buy my usual carton of eggs at the grocery store, I worried I wasn't a good parent. I knew it was irrational, but there were eggs in my refrigerator for my entire life. (They even build the little egg holder into the refrigerator door.) It was one of the first foods I ever fed my baby and one of the first foods I ever cooked for myself as a child. It was strange to stop eating something that was so central to my diet and my culture.

Once I went vegetarian, I heard people call eggs "chicken periods," which didn't make sense to me at first glance. I knew eggs were part of a chicken's reproductive cycle, but they aren't bloody. If you are a woman you know when you're ovulating because you have a discharge with an egg-white consistency. *Wait? What?!* Now, just imagine taking that egg-white discharge and frying it up in a pan. That would be really nasty, right? So why would you eat the mucous secretion of a chicken? Beyond that, there's a whole complicated abuse pattern in the egg industry. Egg-laying chickens produce eggs for about a year or two, much like with milk production among dairy cows. Once they are no longer useful for their reproductive system they are considered "spent" and must be destroyed. Some are simply gassed; some are sold as pet food, some killed for meat. Killing for human consumption is less likely because egg producing chickens are older than younger birds, and the meat is tougher and more gamey. Male chicks are typically ground alive because they have no use in the egg industry.[6]

I know it's hard to relate to the feelings of animals if you don't spend time with them, or you were taught to look at them as beneath you. The New Oxford American dictionary defines speciesism as "the assumption of human superiority leading to the exploitation of animals." That's the way everyone I know grew up. We didn't even necessarily let the dogs in the house.

In my old house we used to get water bugs which completely gross me out. I was a single mom, so I had to kill my own bugs when necessary. I remember chasing down this giant roach, when my daughter screamed, "Mom, it's just trying to run away!" *Really?! My daughter had to bring compassion to a roach extermination?* Well, I learned from my daughter that day. A light went on in me, and, now I do my best to take bugs outside if they get "lost" in my house. There was no denying that bug new *exactly* what he was doing, and he was trying to get the fuck out of my bathroom before he caught some of my bug spray.

For him, it was life or death. For me, it was nothing. It made me think.

If water bugs have an awareness about their own lives, we can surmise that bees and ants have incredibly complicated lives. Through my fascination with butterflies, I learned monarch butterflies migrate 3,000 miles from Canada to Mexico twice a year. We may be bigger and more violent than animals and insects, but we certainly can't fly 3,000 miles without a plane, enter our neighbors' homes through tiny vents or keep the world food supply in symbiosis through pollination. We need them. We should respect them, even if we don't want to live with them.

Some people stop eating meat because they don't like the taste of it, or they want a healthier lifestyle. That wasn't me. I stopped because I woke up to the cruelty and the nastiness that I was financing. It's so disgusting, most people will not watch the film *Earthlings* or Google factory farming images. It's so revolting our sensibilities tell us not to look at it. And, yet, if it's hidden from us and presented on a plate of lies, we will gladly eat it.

Many well-known and admired people have made the decision not to eat animal products as part of a stance against injustice. Martin Luther King Jr. famously said, "Injustice anywhere is a threat to justice everywhere."

Sistah Vegan was the first book I read with my Black Vegan Life™ group in Atlanta. In it there's a poem from Mary Spears called, "Eyes of the Dead" where she says, "The mother cow breastfeeds the human race…my ancestors breastfed the white race…No one could have said to me, 'what's the big deal? It's just an animal.' I could have remembered a time when someone might have said the same about me."

When I first went vegan, I was often triggered in Facebook groups when white people compared animal slavery to human slavery. As Black people we have a long, cruel history of being compared to animals and a collective trauma resulting from centuries of slavery and oppression. It wasn't until I realized deep in my spirit that we all have the same right to exist, that I was able to recognize the atrocities that take place against animals are just as evil as those that take place against humans. I've come to believe it's foundational.

*If we didn't think it was okay
to torture and abuse animals,
we wouldn't graduate to doing the same to people.*

Psychiatrists say psychopaths begin harming animals before they start attacking people.[7] In my lifetime I've seen the portrayal of violence grow in movies and video games. It makes sense that violence has a foundation and needs a path. I don't know how you spend a day killing hundreds of animals and go home, kiss your kids and make love to your partner. The trauma sounds apocalyptic. Slaughterhouse workers are exploited nearly as much as the animals. And violence begets more violence. Where does all that murderous energy go at the end of the work day? Part of me is scared to find out. Part of me thinks I already know. The industry is notorious for employee turnover because of the nastiness of the job. To add insult to injury, the USDA issued a rule in 2019 allowing high-speed slaughter above the limit of 1,106 animals per hour.[8]

*Imagine the opposite of a society
built on violence and inhumanity.
Imagine a world where every soul was self-actualized,
every animal had the right to live,
and all men and women were equal
regardless of race, class or background.*

As Nelson Mandela said, "It always seems impossible until it's done." I remember when Mandela was released from prison in 1990. Apartheid came to an end, and he became the first democratically elected president of the new South Africa four years later. Nothing seemed more impossible than that.

The physical health benefits of a plant-based diet are widely available.
The emotional and spiritual benefits are beyond words.

When I first went vegan, I used to sing a little jingle in my head, "Being vegan makes me happy." It was a reminder that this was a choice that I made out of self-love and compassion. I didn't know it at the time, but it was one of my first affirmations. The jingle helped when I left my house and was confronted with the constant barrage of Burger King's, McDonald's and KFC's that were waiting outside my door. Our language cleverly allows us to take living, breathing, sentient beings and reduce them to inanimate objects like burgers, wings, gelatin or leather. They deserve far more respect than they're given. Their plight resembles that of other oppressed populations whether women or minorities.

Just because we have the power to control, oppress and harm animals doesn't mean that we should.
The Garden of Eden,
God's paradise for people, was vegan.
And, most of the animals we eat are herbivores.

The Vegan Society defines veganism as "a way of living which seeks to exclude, as far as is possible and practicable, all forms of exploitation of, and cruelty to, animals for food, clothing or any other purpose." People often ask me what's the hardest part about going vegan. My answer is always the same – you have to open your mouth and stand up for yourself. You have to learn how to say "no." You have to make a commitment to something larger than you. You have to buck tradition, and perhaps, even authority. Beans and rice are everywhere, recipes are easy to find, and vegan options are available at many fast food chains. Google and YouTube have lots of vegan recipes and even cooking shows. One of my favorites is with Chef Beee. I was even a guest on her show in

2019, where I made a delicious kale salad and fresh-pressed sweet potato juice. (You will not believe how good juiced sweet potatoes are!) If you're in a food desert and don't have access to a lot of variety, Amazon and a host of other companies ship just about everything. It's not about the food – it's about taking a stand.

I understand if now is not the right time for you to make a big change. However, just raising your consciousness around food, animals and the environment is a huge accomplishment. If you decide to go once a week, once a month, or once a year without consuming animal products, it helps. Even if you just change your cosmetics or toiletry brands to vegan products that's a powerful step in the right direction.

Any new realization of the cruel habits we've inherited from our oppressors is worthy of celebration.

Tamika Mallory, co-founder of Until Freedom, really struck a chord with me in her recent speech following the murder of George Floyd. She said, "We learned violence from you."[9] Violence is learned behavior. There are times when violence is necessary, but we don't have to accept it when it's not.

Factory farming is not only destroying our hearts by making us callous to the pain of others, and our bodies by making us more prone to heart disease, diabetes and obesity, it is also destroying the environment. Over 6.7 million acres of tropical forests are destroyed each year for cattle production.[10] These animals produce incomprehensible amounts of waste which are sometimes sprayed onto neighboring areas, often communities of color. This is part of what is known as environmental racism.[11] In factory farms, animals do not reproduce normally. The males are masturbated for semen and the females are artificially inseminated. Nothing about the process is normal or healthy.[12]

Before I went vegan I used to buy free-range eggs and grass-fed beef. I was trying to work through my guilt, by eating "humanely" slaughtered animals. One day a friend of mine said very simply, "There's no humane way to kill someone." Not just a someone, a baby. According to clearlyveg.com, chickens are slaughtered at six weeks old, pigs and lambs at about six months, and cows at about two years old. Dairy cows are repeatedly inseminated and impregnated on what is aptly named a "rape rack." When they give birth, both their babies and their milk are stolen until they are finally killed at about five years old. The more I learned, the more I couldn't justify what I was doing. I imagined pretty white ladies in fancy dresses in the 1800's drinking sweet tea and pretending they didn't know their husband was raping their enslaved workers. I couldn't play mind tricks to get myself out of this one.

I hosted a retreat for my Black Vegan Life™ group back in 2017 at a beautiful resort in the North Georgia mountains. Most of the participants were either vegan, vegetarian, pescatarian or something along the path of more conscious eating. A good friend of mine, who wasn't vegan, attended. It was the only three days in her life that she'd gone without dairy. She was shocked by how good she felt and never ate dairy again. Our culture says we're lactose-intolerant as if it's a defect. Adult mammals are not supposed to drink breastmilk throughout our adult lives. Particularly not breastmilk from another species. We are supposed to WEAN, like every other mammal.

We have been so brainwashed by the meat and dairy industries; we don't believe we can survive without those dietary elements. I know I considered them staples. They were not the staples of our African ancestors.

As we reclaim our heritage, we can reclaim a diet that is healthier for our bodies and our minds. We can move away from violence and reclaim our compassion.

Now my staples are things like almond milk, black beans, chickpeas, sweet potatoes, kale, dates, bananas, avocados, brown rice, quinoa, oats, nuts, rice noodles, nutritional yeast and raw sauerkraut. Nothing is more joyful.

Some folks worry about nutrition. There are innumerable sources that state a whole food, plant-based diet provides optimal nutrition for humans. Because of the depletion of our soil we should all take a B-12 supplement. We can either take it directly or we can ingest it through the meat of animals who have been given supplementation. When we eat meat, we consume not only the B-12 fed to the animal, but also the antibiotics they receive to survive their filthy living conditions.

Stealing eggs from chickens or milk from cows is still stealing. Eating someone's body or wearing their skin is the biggest theft of all. Intersectionality is a term used to describe the point where multiple systems of oppression meet. Webster defines it as "the complex, cumulative way in which the effects of multiple forms of discrimination (such as racism, sexism, and classism) combine, overlap or intersect especially in the experiences of marginalized individuals or groups." In the Webster definition we can easily insert speciesism. I see it as the way systematic oppression hinders me as both a Black person and as a woman, and this same system tortures and sexually assaults animals, especially female animals. This same system oppresses the slaughterhouse workers who are typically minorities and often immigrants.[13]

I care about everyone. I cannot joyfully benefit from harming others, especially if they are the most innocent and defenseless among us. Treating others the way we want to be treated is the foundation of compassion. Benefiting from harming others is simply not the way goddesses roll. If you want to really be happy, let it go.

Affirmations for Compassion:
- ❖ I am the result of what I consume physically, mentally and spiritually.
- ❖ Everyone's life is precious.
- ❖ I forgive you. I hope that you forgive me.
  (Repeat at least 2x per day.)

Reflection Questions:
- ❖ Do you feel any differently about sex work and other occupations or crimes of desperation?
- ❖ How do you feel about what you've learned about animal agriculture practices in the United States?
- ❖ How do you feel about the current level of compassion in your life?

Time to Get Still:
- ❖ Choose your own stillness practice this week, or visit TrishAhjelRoberts.com/resources and access Meditation #10 for Compassion.
  (Enjoy at least 2x per week, but daily is ideal.)

Let's Pollinate!
- ❖ Make a commitment to elevate your level of compassion for others. Consider addressing social justice initiatives, environmentalism, intersectionality, and goals related to reducing cruelty and oppression.
- ❖ Set a SMART goal: Specific, Measurable, Attainable, emotionally Relevant and Timebound.
- ❖ Continue to work with your accountability partner.

Grooves for Fluttering:

- Marvin Gaye. "Mercy, Mercy Me (The Ecology)." *What's Going On?* 1971.
- Stic.Man of Dead Prez. "Healthy Livin'." *The Workout,* 2011.
- Earth, Wind & Fire. "Shining Star." *That's the Way of the World,* 1975.
- The 5th Dimension. "Aquarius/Let the Sun Shine In." *The Age of Aquarius,* 1969.

Think-Through Films:

- *Food Inc.* Directed by Robert Kenner. Starring Eric Schlosser. Dogwoof Pictures, 2008.
- *We Are One.* Directed by Kevin Mukherji. Featuring Forest Whitaker. Carlos Sanz Production, 2017.
- *The Game Changers.* Directed by Louie Psihoyos. Starring James Wilks. Game Changers Film, 2019.
- *The Post-Traumatic Slave Diet.* Featuring Dr. Milton Mills. Karen Boone Production, 2016.
- *Vegucated.* Directed by Marisa Miller Wolfson. Starring Tesla Lobo. Get Vegucated, 2011.
- *Cowspiracy: The Sustainability Secret.* Directed by Kip Anderson. Starring Kip Anderson. Appian Way, 2016.
- *Lovelace.* Directed by Rob Epstein. Starring Amanda Seyfried. Nu Image, 2013.
- *Hair.* Directed by Miloš Forman. Starring Treat Williams. CIP Filmproduktion, 1979.
- *Earthlings.* Directed by Shaun Monson. Narrated by Joaquin Phoenix. Nation Earth, 2005.
- *Fat, Sick and Nearly Dead.* Directed by Joe Cross. Featuring Joe Cross. Gravitas Ventures, 2010.

Additional Resources:
- TrishAhjelRoberts.com/resources is your main portal for all resources.
- *Sistah Vegan*. Edited by A. Breeze Harper
- *The Happy Vegan* by Russell Simmons
- *By Any Greens Necessary* by Tracye Lynn McQuirter
- *Skinny Bitch* by Rory Freedman
- *Addict Nation: An Intervention for America* by Jane Velez-Mitchell
- *Let Plants Nourish You* by D. Natasha "Chef Beee" Brewley
- *ChefBeee.com*
- *Veganize and Heal Your Life* by Neeta Sanders
- *The Prevent and Reverse Heart Disease Cookbook* by Ann Crile Esselstyn and Jane Esselstyn
- *Heal Thyself for Health and Longevity* by Queen Afua
- *The Greenprint: Plant-Based Diet, Best Body, Better World* by Marco Borges
- Africanamericanveganstarterguide.com/
- *Universal Compassion* by Gelse Kelsang Gyatso
- Peta.org/living/food/african-americans-animal-rights/
- Vegansociety.com
- 22daysnutrition.com
- Purplecarrot.com
- Amazon, Audible, YouTube, Google and your local library

Eleventh Drop: Work Equals Play

"I would rather die of passion than of boredom."
- Vincent Van Gogh

_____
_____
_____
_____

Welcome to the other side. The hardest work is over. This is where we really begin to enjoy the seeds that we've planted. We are softened by newfound compassion, awakened to the sweetness of present moments, surrendered to the Divine flow of life, released of attachments, opened to generosity, freed from anger, and embraced by authenticity and self-love. We have created community and support, nurtured our inner spirit and healed past trauma. We are not 100%. We know this is a journey, but we can see the light at the end of the tunnel, and we've had moments of sheer bliss.

What does a life well-lived really look like? Is it our parents' lives or those of celebrities we admire? Is it season tickets to a sports arena, a well-stocked wine cellar, or an athletically toned body? Perhaps it's just sleeping well at night and dancing in the mirror in the mornings? Or maybe a Cinderella love story followed by life in a castle? Or, is it traveling the world with a backpack and eating cupcakes all the way? You've probably heard the old adage: when you do what you love you'll never work a day in your life. I know I heard it my whole life and never believed it. It wasn't something I heard from my parents. It was poetic dreaming, nothing meant to be taken seriously. As much as I've been called a free spirit and a free-thinker, I still believed in following the rules, staying the course and playing it safe. Black women weren't supposed to take the risks that others could. I got the degrees I believed I needed to make sure I was always employable. Now I've seen a YouTube video go viral with an unemployed Black woman who graduated from Harvard. It shows me that there are no guarantees and no barriers. I'm a big fan of my adopted-daughter-in-my-head Cardi B, who's shown the world how to create her own market with nearly seventy million Instagram followers.

Now is our time to dream together.
What if you could get paid to do work you're passionate about that also serves the world?

I'm inspired by women like Patrisse Khan-Cullors, Alicia Garza and Opal Tometi who founded the Black Lives Matter organization in 2013. I'm deeply impressed with activists like Tamika Mallory and Shaun King who shine light on our stories. These are people who work with passion and purpose toward goals that help all of us.

Formal education is valuable, but there is no replacement for ACTION. I am very grateful I've had the opportunity to earn two degrees. I love school and am considering pursuing an MFA next. I've always had a love for learning, and I appreciate the structure that formal education offers, whether it's a certificate or a degree program.

Sexism and racism are around every corner and behind most doors. A solid primary education is profoundly important, and advanced credentials are just more tools in your toolbox.

If you can gain access to accredited degree or certificate programs without incurring significant debt, it's well worth the investment. I started working full-time at the age of seventeen. I taught myself to type thinking I would always be able to get a job. This was back in the '80s, and it never occurred to me I could be employed but not able to support myself. I later worked as an administrative assistant at large corporate headquarters in New York City for a top cosmetics company, and later, a major financial firm. I went to night school for my bachelor's, with partial reimbursement from my employer. Once I got my degree, I was able to move into professional marketing and sales roles that would have been closed to me otherwise. I thought if I had sales skills, I could always get a job. As young and privileged as I was, living in one of the most prestigious cities in the world, I was operating from a place of scarcity and desperation.

Throughout my work history I often felt underemployed. I was never able to use all of my talents. I knew the white men who hired me checked boxes on their to-do list while simultaneously putting me in whatever box was most convenient. I knew I was supposed to play the corporate game, but I've never liked straight lines, and I wasn't interested in the box or the game. There was a part of me that felt like a round peg in a square hole. I never quite fit the corporate matrix, being neither political nor competitive – I wanted everyone to win. And, there was a part of sales that always felt disingenuous and fearmongering. People often make decisions from a place of fear, but I never felt good as its proponent.

I hesitantly moved into sales at a telecom firm, where I spent seven years. It wasn't long before I became disillusioned by the institutionalized racism and questionable integrity surrounding me, I left to work for a college before finally purchasing a fitness franchise. I thought I had found a way to make my work equal play.

When I moved to Atlanta I worked as a financial advisor for twelve years. I am fascinated by the global economy, and I enjoyed the work, but I was consistently underpaid and overstressed. After years of pursuing hobbies, creating community and developing my spiritual life, I realized I needed to break out of my shell. *Why was I working so hard toward someone else's dream without even being appropriately compensated for my efforts? Why was I so scared all the time?* I was scared of being homeless, embarrassed or losing my moderate social standing and the right to call myself "middle-class." I was scared to lose footing on this wobbly economic and social structure that had become the remains of my American Dream. Something shifted in me. I had to make a decision.

> **Did I want to live just a little or a lot?**
> **Was I doing my best work,**
> **or was I just playing it safe?**

There's a quote that I love from the late poet, Mary Oliver, "Are you breathing just a little and calling it a life?" I realized my work was keeping me from living with the purpose I imagined for my life. I tried to bring my passion for helping others to my role as a financial advisor by focusing on socially responsible investing. Ultimately, I had to accept the fact I had chosen the wrong work. I chose it because it was interesting, but also because I thought it was safe. Surely adding a Series 7 designation to my MBA would make me even more attractive to employers. It was as if I was doing the employee version of Match.com on my LinkedIn profile. I'm smart, I'm pretty, I've got a great personality and look at this laundry list of degrees and certifications. I even run marathons. *Don't you want to date/hire/cherish me?!* There's a '70s song lyric from "Do What You Wanna Do" by the Dramatics – "The strong give up and move on; the weak give up and stay." I had to go. I just had a big birthday, and this couldn't be the apex of my life – doing work and not being appreciated, dreading Mondays, and having phony relationships with co-workers.

I gave myself permission to dream. It was terrifying but necessary. I didn't have to actually change anything, I assured myself. I just had to imagine some possibilities. Finding the courage to dream was incredibly difficult. Since then, I have created "Courage to Dream" workshops to help others through the process.

> **I was shocked to realize how long it had been since I had allowed myself to dream.**
> **I was so busy staying on the track that was laid out for me, my dream muscle was completely atrophied.**

The thoughts flooded my mind. I couldn't sleep. *Suppose I quit my job? How would I survive?* I could teach yoga and take on coaching clients. I could take on a roommate. I could host more retreats and do some freelance writing. *What was I willing to give up?* I finally decided that I was willing to give everything up. My daughter was going off to college, so the timing was good. If I had to sell my house and couch-surf to pursue my dream, I could do it without dragging her along with me. If I had to move back into my parents' house, I could. I would do what I needed to do, and if I failed, I would die trying. I had been laying the foundation for years. Now was the time to make a move.

I used to joke about being on the "struggle bus" as an exhausted, underpaid single mom. I didn't realize I was telling the Universe what I expected. Now, I tell people, I'm on the bus. I'm not driving this thing. I don't even want to. The Universe leads me, and my job is not to fight it and not to complain. Part of what was so exhausting was always trying to control outcomes. I can't control end results any more than I can control the weather. Now, I work in the flow. When I'm sleeping, doing yoga, taking a walk or in meditation, ideas arise from the clarity of my mind. I'm always prepared to jot them down. (I have over 1,000 note pages in my iPhone. A little crazy, I know.) I live in gratitude, and I work for the greater good, so I cannot go wrong.

Letting go of my house wasn't easy. I spent the past twenty years as a homeowner. However, there's not a single possession that I have ever owned that is more valuable than my dream of "work equals play." Now, I wake up in the morning with gratitude and purpose. I'm playing, doing work that I would do for free.

Work equaling play doesn't mean you can't be a waiter or a street-sweeper. It does mean you do work you genuinely enjoy that challenges you.

I'm sure you're familiar with Martin Luther King Jr.'s famous quote, "If a man is called to be a street sweeper…he should sweep the streets so well that all the hosts of heaven and earth will pause to say, 'here lived a great street sweeper who did his job well.'" If you think sweeping streets isn't challenging work, give it a try. It's as important as any job. In his masterpiece, *The Prophet,* Kahlil Gibran says, "Work is love made visible."

Even simple and seemingly mundane work can be challenging and done with love and passion. When I lived in Brooklyn, I often drove through a busy intersection near where the Barclays Center is now. There was a traffic cop out there, no matter the weather, dancing while he directed traffic with a smile. You could see his joy and his flow. I was fortunate to have a housekeeper who told me she loved cleaning. She would clean my home until it shone and sparkled, listening to music and smiling. She was in the zone.

I realize not everyone is in a position to quit their job and become an actor, a singer or a comedian, for example. *Or can they?* We cling to a perception of safety that isn't actually real. We think if we have the house, the car, the spouse or the stuff we will be protected from pain, when, in reality, the pain will greet us regardless of the lavish gates we build to avoid it. In the meantime, how should we live our lives? Should we hoard our fear along with our sweaters, old shoes and paperback books? Now don't go running to work in the morning to quit your job. I will not be paying your bills. However, as you release attachments to things, you may find your life becomes more spacious and flexible, and then, who knows what shifts may come your way.

Changing jobs or pursuing self-employment are only a couple of ways to make work equal play in your life. You might reinvent your existing job, like the traffic cop or the housekeeper, adding enthusiasm or additional creativity into what you're already doing. By creating a positive aura, you will attract opportunities you can't even imagine. You can also find volunteer work that brings you joy and improves your skills or knowledge in an area of interest. Volunteer work can be a great option if you're retired or unemployed as a bridge to a new career.

Even if you're working full-time, finding a few hours a week to focus on your passions is crucial.

Recently I was working on a major holiday and didn't even realize it. I know part of my disconnection was from the mental muddiness of quarantine life, but part was just from being in "the zone." Most of my adult life has been planned around national holidays and vacation days. Even when I worked autonomously at jobs I enjoyed, I had to follow a schedule and promote a dream that wasn't my own. When I worked for companies that had me sick with the Sunday flu, Mondays were like re-entry from the frying pan back into the fire. Tuesdays were even worse after a long weekend, as if having a glimpse of freedom only intensified the pain.

Nowadays, I can work twelve hours without realizing how much time has passed. From when I first pad into my kitchen to make my green tea latte in the morning until I click away at my laptop in my bed. I love it. I get lost in it. Creating beautiful content to share with you brings me so much joy.

One thing that hindered my first attempt at self-employment was the inability to distinguish between services I liked to receive and work that I wanted to do. For example, I love receiving massages, so much so I considered getting my massage therapist license. Then, I realized, I didn't think I would enjoy touching strangers hour after hour. Part of the reason I opened my fitness center was because I really enjoyed working out and wanted to create a space for other women in my community. The reality was it's nearly impossible to workout at your own gym, and I didn't like opening and closing. I enjoyed teaching classes, talking to the women and inspiring them, but the day-to-day schedule wasn't my thing.

*If you consider making a change,
speak to women who look like you,
who have done what you are contemplating.*

I recently spoke to a couple of young Black women who were considering careers as financial advisors in Atlanta. I gave them an earful. They will ultimately make their own decisions, but now they have the benefit of a woman who is experienced in that field. In my first few years as a financial advisor, I knew the industry wasn't healthy for me. I became obsessed with an old children's book, *Harold and the Purple Crayon*. In the story Harold is a little boy with a big purple crayon who is literally able to draw his own world. When he was nervous, and his hand started to shake, he accidentally drew an ocean that almost drowned him. Through the metaphor in the book I came to understand that I was drawing my own life. I made many small decisions every moment and many big ones over the years which brought me to my present moment. Even when I didn't think I was making a decision and I was paralyzed with fear, my inaction was actually a decision, and I had to take responsibility for it. This is not to say that I wasn't the recipient of all kinds of prejudice and inequality – if you're a Black woman, you know that's par for the course. I just had to take responsibility for my share.

*Now, I am living in the zone, completely immersed
in my dream of global self-actualization
beginning with Black women.*

I've been asked, why Black women? This is the deal. I used to volunteer with a microfinance charity. If you're not familiar with the term, microfinancing is when a small loan is given to an individual or business, typically in a developing country. For example, you might loan $50 to a woman in Somalia or Indonesia to start a tailoring business or open a fruit stand. Because women are historically marginalized, and have more responsibility for keeping the family fed, sheltered and educated, when women win, we all win. Microfinance firms often target women for that reason. Black women, with our dubious reign as "double minorities," and thus, double marginalization are "the mules of the world," as expressed by Zora Neale Hurston in one of my all-time favorite books, *Their Eyes Were Watching God.* We are the mother of humankind and the foundation of the earth. When our tide swells, all ships rise.

I remember when I first whispered my dream in my blog, "The Secret Weapon," in October 2019. A few weeks later, I spoke the words to a friend from my book club. Finally, instead of deciding the dream was too big to come true, I gave it wings. *Who am I to say what is and isn't possible?* Babies are created from a single cell. The sun is ninety-four million miles from the earth. The oceans follow the call of the moon. My body is capable of fighting infection, writing this book, listening to the rain, and following its circadian rhythm simultaneously. My mayor's name is Keisha, and three Black women started a global movement called Black Lives Matter.

I'm not convinced anything is impossible.

From this place of dreaming, of doing good and wanting better I more often than not find myself working in "the zone." According to Huffpost.com, being in the zone or "flow" is a state of heightened focus and blissful immersion.[1] Cambridge dictionary defines "in the zone" as "happy or excited because you are doing something very skillfully and easily." I agree with both. The only pain in the zone is the inability to stop, or the trouble of getting back in the zone after a disruption.

I'm doing work that I don't want to take a vacation from. Is this how Ava DuVernay feels when she's wrapped up in a new film? Or Missy Elliot working on a new track? Serena delivering a backhand? Misty Copeland in pirouette? I think this is what Van Gogh meant in his quote at the beginning of this drop, "I'd rather die of passion than of boredom."

We all have to die, what better reason than passion?

I hope you're spending some time in the zone. If you're not, here are a few tips:

- ❖ Think of the last time you were really enjoying yourself without alcohol or any other intoxicants, what were you doing? (Sex doesn't count. Lol. Although, I'm all for the sex zone.)
- ❖ Think about the items on your bucket list that you haven't checked off yet. (If you don't have a bucket list, consider making one.)
- ❖ Think about your dream job if you didn't have to make a living. What would you do? (Don't be cautious, really dream!)
- ❖ Think about trauma or difficulty from your past that you can use for something positive. (Who are you uniquely qualified to help?)

Now take this list and fly with it. Even if it's only a couple of hours a week, set aside some time to research your bucket list, pursue those joy-inducing activities, your dream job or helping someone learn from your past hurts. **That's zone material.** Once you play in that sandbox you'll never want to leave.

Affirmations for Passion:
- ❖ I am uniquely qualified for a job only I can do.
- ❖ I enjoy sharing my gifts with the world.
- ❖ I love when I'm joyfully working and flowing in the zone.

    (Repeat at least 2x per day.)

Reflection Questions:
- ❖ How do you feel about your level of joy with your occupation? What can you do to improve it?
- ❖ How often do you feel like you're in the zone?

Time to Get Still:
- ❖ Choose your own stillness practice this week, or visit TrishAhjelRoberts.com/resources and access Meditation #11 for Passion.

    (Enjoy at least 2x per week, but daily is ideal.)

Let's Pollinate!
- ❖ Make a commitment to increase the play and passion in your work life.
- ❖ Set a SMART goal: Specific, Measurable, Attainable, emotionally Relevant and Timebound.
- ❖ Continue to work with your accountability partner.

Grooves for Fluttering:
- ❖ Rihanna. "Work." *Anti*, 2016.
- ❖ Ciara. "Level Up." *Level Up*, 2018.
- ❖ Destiny's Child. "Independent Woman." *Survivor*, 2001.
- ❖ Sampa the Great. "Black Girl Magik." *Birds and the BEE9*, 2017.

Think-Through Films:
- *Self Made: Inspired by the Life of Madam CJ Walker.* Directed by Kasi Lemmons. Starring Octavia Spencer and Tiffany Haddish. Spring Hill Entertainment, 2020.
- *A Ballerina's Tale.* Directed by Nelson George. Starring Misty Copeland. Urban Romances Inc., 2015.
- *The Banker.* Directed by George Nolfi. Starring Anthony Mackie. Apple TV, 2020.
- *Harriet.* Directed by Kasi Lemmons. Starring Cynthia Erivo. Perfect World Pictures, 2019.
- *Ali.* Directed by Michael Mann. Starring Will Smith. Columbia Pictures, 2001.

Additional Resources:
- TrishAhjelRoberts.com/resources is your main portal for all resources.
- Blacklivesmatter.com
- Untilfreedom.com
- Grassrootslaw.org
- *Have You Ever Tried to Enter the Long Black Branches?* by Mary Oliver (poem)
- *What Color is Your Parachute?* by Richard N. Bolles
- *Harold and the Purple Crayon* by Crockett Johnson
- *The Prophet* by Kahlil Gibran
- Amazon, Audible, YouTube, Google and your local library

Twelfth Drop: Float Like a Butterfly

> "I am the greatest.
> I said that even before I knew I was."
> - Muhammad Ali

_____
_____
_____
_____

Here we are. I'm over here feeling like Mother Nature gazing on a rosebud. I hope you can feel the love. We've arrived. This drop is about remembering all that we are and all that we've become. It's about nurturing and enjoying the sweet fullness and miracle of being a human, especially as a Black woman. We are magic.

I love the quote at the beginning of this drop, because long before affirmations became part of the language of popular self-help culture, Muhammad Ali had the foresight to tell the world he was the greatest of all time. That takes courage. I'm sure he had moments of doubt, we all do, but he did the work, stuck to his story and watched it manifest.

I love the imagery of the floating butterfly. Its movements seem effortless because it's going with the flow of the air and its own unique abilities. In other words, it's flowing with life. When you look closely, you may notice the butterfly doesn't flap its wings – its wings are really too big to flap. Rather, it contracts its body and makes a figure eight with them. And yes, if you were at the dancehall club back in the day listening to Beenie Man and doing "the butterfly," it's the same movement. The butterfly's been dancing all along, and we can too. Dancing while we heal and work. Dancing in community, generosity, compassion and spirit. Dancing in authenticity and self-love. Dancing while letting go and while waiting. Dancing while we create our vision.

2020 has been a difficult year for many of us. Besides the impact on our mental and physical health from isolation, we bear the brunt of the economic fallout and the continued brutality against Black people in the U.S. The rage overflows and destroys our physical and mental health, our families and our communities. The decision to be joyful is, exactly that, a decision. I know if you don't have food, shelter or safety, dancing won't be your first priority. I know when you have lost a loved one, especially through violence, the trauma is deep and the scars linger. I pray that you find healing not only in my words, but in the tools that I've shared with you. I hope you can see some light at the end of the long tunnel.

> *Our ancestors sang in the cotton fields*
> *even under threat of the whip.*
> *Sometimes our joy is the only thing*
> *that can't be stolen from us.*

When we first started together, I talked about having a "think-through," recognizing that life could be different and preparing for an internal shift. So much of our culture focuses on our external appearance: our hair, skin, nails, height, weight and features. I hope you've experienced a movement within your own heart.

It's easier to dance when you have hope. When you have a roadmap. When you know what your passions are. When you've identified the things that make you happy. I hope you've found some, if not all of that here. When the sparks from various think-throughs come together and connect, *Bam!* – the breakthrough can happen. Maybe you've felt the explosion, maybe not. It's huge and it takes time. It may happen as one big blast or many small ones. Either way, you'll know it when you feel it.

From the day we are born, society tells us whether we should be dressed in pink or blue, if we should drink our mother's milk or a concoction from someone else's mother, what and whose body we should eat, what we need to know, what we should believe, where we can live, who we can love, and on and on. Our society tells us who we are and who it thinks we should be.

When we learn to follow our own innate set of skills, talents and passions, we learn to float. Life gets easier. Goals become attainable. As we've learned in the drops, we can't fly with a brick on our back – there are things we need to release to truly soar. We have to heal from our past traumas, stop harming ourselves and others, and let go of anger, attachment and greed. In this releasing we discover that we feel *good*.

We reach toward the things that will raise our consciousness and make us feel even better: recognizing our own unique spirit, creating community, learning to love our authentic self, expanding our generosity, asking for help, developing patience and working with joy and enthusiasm.

Now's the time to pull everything together into a sustainable self-love and self-care practice that you can enjoy for many years. If you've worked through the activities you've already had a lot of practice. Regular meditation and time for stillness and reflection, affirmations and journaling are powerful tools. I have four journals at my bedside. I don't write in them every night, only when I get the urge, but I try to be consistent. One is a traditional journal where I can keep track of day-to-day activities and accomplishments. The second one is a gratitude journal – I write at least three things that I'm grateful for every day. The third is a place to record my dreams and what I think my subconscious mind is telling me in my sleep. My fourth is my *Live in Wonder* journal which I've been writing in for the past five years. Apps make it easy to access some wonderful resources for meditation, yoga nidra, affirmations and journaling. I very rarely go back and read my journals, unless I'm looking for something. When I do it's always interesting. We all have stories to share and emotions to process. Writing helps us harness our thoughts from fleeting indistinguishable clouds to something more concrete and actionable. Many times when pen hits the paper I'm surprised by what comes out of me. Just like the butterfly, I let it flow.

If you've never tried yoga, now is a great time to start. One thing quarantine has given us is lots of online content to choose from. There's a wide range of free and low-cost online yoga classes in varying modalities for all levels. Chair yoga, restorative, yin and gentle flow are generally accessible to everyone. Power yoga is probably best left in the studio where you have more guidance, or for experienced yoga practitioners. My favorite online offering nowadays is with Jaimee Ratliff, here in Atlanta. You can purchase yoga props and practice at home, or just grab a blanket and get on the floor. Yoga existed long before yoga mats were invented. Just be safe. Yoga should *always* feel good. If it doesn't feel good, ease up. Tomorrow is another day.

Take care of your body. We can't break out of our chrysalis if we're damaging ourselves with alcohol, tobacco, drugs, poor nutrition or lack of rest. Being a Black woman is already stressful, we need to be extra good to ourselves. In my free e-book, *Black Vegan Life*™ *Guide to Self-Care*, I offer additional guidance. I'd love for you to sign-up for the e-book and my weekly inspirational blog. Don't let this be the last time we connect. I have so much more to share with you.

Now it's time to enjoy the sweetness of life. Improving every day and forgiving ourselves when we stumble. Speaking kindly to ourselves even if we're the only person to do so. Taking baths. Taking naps. Anointing ourselves with fragrant and essential oils. Knowing we're good and worthy. Living without guilt or regrets. Feeling the warmth of a loving heart each morning when we rise. This is life on the other side of the chrysalis.

You may think this is a lot. With all the day-to-day demands of work and family, who has time for all of this? You know what? You're right. It is a lot. When we started together, I said you might work through a drop per month or a drop per year. I wasn't kidding. Even if you only work on one drop and never do another, it can profoundly improve the quality of your life. Choose one that resonates with you and start from there. Personal growth is about joy and fulfillment. Just like the butterfly, it might seem like some of us are easily floating, but many of us put in the work when we were caterpillars to create the illusion of effortless flight.

I no longer worry about the things I used to, but I'm still a human in a world of problems. I forgive myself when I fall short. We all fall short. I've learned to live in light outside the chrysalis. I hope you will too!

Affirmations for Freedom:
- There are infinite possibilities in my life.
- I live a life without limits.
- Every day of my life is a new creation waiting to unfold.
  (Repeat at least 2x per day.)

Reflection Questions:
- How do you feel about your level of ease and fulfillment in life?
- Do you feel like you experienced *aha!* moments, a think-through or even a breakthrough in the course of this book?

Time to Get Still:
- Choose your own stillness practice this week.
  (Enjoy at least 2x per week, but daily is ideal.)

Let's Pollinate!
- Make a commitment to share what you've learned with others.

Grooves for Fluttering:
- Pharrell Williams. "Freedom." (single) 2015.
- Inner City. "Good Life." *Big Fun,* 1989.
- Stic.Man of Dead Prez. "Yoga Mat." *The Workout,* 2011.
- Deniece Williams. "Black Butterfly." *Let's Hear it for the Boy,* 1984.

Think-Through Films:
- All movies require conflict. Characters must have adversaries. It's time to graduate from the drama! If you want to see a film showing ease, create a video of you doing your version of the butterfly dance! Please post in Black Girl Butterflyz on Facebook. It will create a fun way for us to introduce ourselves. Don't worry, I'll post mine too!

Additional Resources:
- TrishAhjelRoberts.com/resources is your main portal for all resources.
- *Live In Wonder: A Journal of Quests, Quotes, & Questions to Jumpstart Your Journey* by Eric Saperson with Mirabella Love
- *Mind-Blowing Happiness™ Guide to Self-Care (e-book)* by Trish Ahjel Roberts available at TrishAhjelRoberts.com.
- JaimeeRatliff.com
- Stellar-PowerYoga.com
- Stic.Man of Dead Prez. *The Workout.* (album) 2011.
- Beenie Man. "Do the Butterfly." *Ruff 'n' Tuff,* 1999
- Amazon, Audible, YouTube, Google and your local library

Questions for Your Kaleidoscope

1) In what ways did you relate to the author's story of healing? Do you think mental health gets enough attention among your family and friends?

2) What was your take on the author's spiritual journey? Did it make you think about your own spiritual path any differently?

3) What are some of the ways you've built your own support network? Do you think your network is diverse and strong enough?

4) How do you feel about your own masks and uniforms? Do you agree with the author's assertion that we have a crisis of authenticity? Explain.

5) What would a world without anger look like to you? Do you think it would be boring or wonderful? Do you believe you can be hurt and outraged and move straight into action without dwelling in anger?

6) Who is the most generous person you know? Do you think this person is genuinely happy?

7) Are there people or things in your life that you can loosen your mental and physical grip on to be happier?
8) What did you think of the author's story of her three vision boards? Have you ever made a "craft project" instead of a true vision board?
9) What's your favorite thing to do when you have to wait somewhere?
10) How did you feel about the author's discussion of veganism, speciesism and intersectionality? Did you think it was appropriate for a book about personal development?
11) Do you think it's possible for everyone to find work they can do with enjoyment?
12) Which drop(s) resonated the most with you? How do you plan to continue to use the book in your life? Which strategies do you plan to implement on a regular basis?
13) Did you use any of the resources provided? Which ones?
14) Uplifting music isn't as common in the Black community today as it was during the civil rights movement of the '60s. Why do you think that is?
15) Do you plan to follow this author online or sign-up for her blog? Are you interested in future books and events?

HOW DID

THINKING OUTSIDE THE CHRYSALIS

CHANGE YOUR LIFE?

Share your story for the chance to win a FREE gift!

Email: hello@trishahjelroberts.com

Winners drawn monthly.

Subscribe to

The Mind-Blowing Happiness™ Podcast

For weekly topics, tips and inspiration to juice up your life's journey!

BRING

THE POWER OF TRANSFORMATION

TO YOUR ORGANIZATION

Invite Trish Ahjel Roberts
to speak at your event!

Visit TrishAhjelRoberts.com/Speaking

Follow Trish Ahjel Roberts on social media!

IG: @trishahjelroberts
FB: @trishahjelroberts
Twitter: @trishahjel
YouTube: Trish Ahjel Roberts

About the Author

Trish Ahjel Roberts has made it her mission to inspire and empower you to live with passion and purpose to reach your fullest potential. She is a self-actualization coach, yoga and meditation instructor, reiki practitioner, plant-based retreat organizer and founder of Mind-Blowing Happiness LLC and Black Vegan Life™. She was born and raised in Brooklyn, NY and attended Stuyvesant High School in Manhattan. She holds a bachelor's degree from the Metropolitan College of New York and an MBA from Long Island University. After years of working as a financial advisor with many unhappy, but wealthy, clients, she quit her corporate job to share her 12-step approach to a self-actualized life. She is the author of three self-help books: the e-book, *Mind-Blowing Happiness™ Guide to Self-Care;* th*e* self-help memoir, *Thinking Outside the Chrysalis: A Black Woman's Guide to Spreading Her Wings;* and the inspirational journal, *12 Steps to Mind-Blowing Happiness: A Journal of Insights, Quotes & Questions to Juice Up Your Journey.* She is also the author of the #sexyfunnysmart romantic drama, *Chocolate Soufflé.* She has more than a decade of Buddhist study at Kadampa Meditation Center in Atlanta, GA and has practiced yoga for more than twenty years. She lives with her daughter and their dog, @vegan_cavachon, in Atlanta and travels the world helping people amplify their voice, open their heart and step into their power. She believes movement and nature are therapy and loves hiking, running, hot yoga and anything on the beach.

Notes

Preparing the Caterpillar:
1. Jari Tanner. Author, "Finland Again Tops List of Happiest Nations, US Ranking Drops," AP, 2019. https://www.pbs.org/newshour/economy/finland-again-tops-list-of-happiest-nations-u-s-ranking-drops
2. E.J. Mundell. Author, "Antidepressant Use Soars 65% in 15 Years," CBS News, 2017. https://www.cbsnews.com/news/antidepressant-use-soars-65-percent-in-15-years/

Drop 1:
1. Janeen Sanders. Author. "12 Confronting Statistics on Child Sexual Abuse Statistics All Parents Need to Know," Huffington Post, 2017. https://www.huffpost.com/entry/12-confronting-statistics-on-child-sexual-abuse_b_587dab01e4b0740488c3de49
2. National Coalition Against Domestic Violence, 2020. https://ncadv.org/statistics#:~:text=1%20in%203%20women%20and,be%20considered%20%22domestic%20violence.%22&text=1%20in%207%20women%20and,injured%20by%20an%20intimate%20partner.
3. Fabina Franco, PhD. Author. "Complex Trauma: Dissociation, Fragmentation and Self Understanding," Psych Central, 2018. https://psychcentral.com/lib/dissociation-fragmentation-and-self-understanding/

Drop 2:
1. Jess Blumberg. Author. "A Brief History of the Salem Witch Trials," Smithsonian Magazine, 2007. https://www.smithsonianmag.com/history/a-brief-history-of-the-salem-witch-trials-175162489/
2. History.com Editors. "The Bible," History.com, 2019. https://www.history.com/topics/religion/bible

Drop 7:
1. CDC data. "Life Expectancy at Birth." 2016. https://www.cdc.gov/nchs/data/hus/2017/015.pdf
2. CDC data. "Antidepressant Use in Persons Aged 12 and Over." 2011. https://www.cdc.gov/nchs/products/databriefs/db76.htm
3. NIH Data. "Alcohol Facts and Statistics." 2018. https://www.niaaa.nih.gov/publications/brochures-and-fact-sheets/alcohol-facts-and-statistics
4. NIH Data. "10 Percent of US Adults Have Drug Use Disorder at Some Point in Their Lives." 2015. https://www.nih.gov/news-events/news-releases/10-percent-us-adults-have-drug-use-disorder-some-point-their-lives

Drop 8:
1. Priyanka A. Abhang, Author, "Technological Basics of EEG Recording and Operation of Apparatus," Science Direct, 2016. https://www.sciencedirect.com/topics/agricultural-and-biological-sciences/brain-waves
2. Tris Thorp, Author, "Higher States of Consciousness," Chopra, 2016. http://chopra.com/sites/default/files/Tris_Higher%20States%202016.pdf
3. Tamara L. Goldsby, PhD, Author, "Effects of Singing Bowl Sound Meditation on Mood, Tension, and Well-being," National Institutes of Health, 2016. https://www.ncbi.nlm.nih.gov/pmc/articles/PMC5871151/

Drop 10:
1. Luke 6:31; Matthew 25:40; Matthew 22:39. Holy Bible. New Testament.

2. Edith Honan. Author. "Judge Trims Dog's $12 Million Inheritance," Reuters. 2008. https://www.reuters.com/article/us-helmsley-dog/judge-trims-dogs-12-million-inheritance-idUSN1634773920080616
3. Linda Lowen. Author. "Physical Abuse of Prostitutes is Common," Thoughtco. 2019. https://www.thoughtco.com/prostitution-statistics-rape-physical-abuse-3534139
4. Megan Turner. Author, "Is This Art?" NY Post, 1999. https://nypost.com/1999/09/21/is-this-art-butchered-animals-a-dung-smeared-virgin-mary-and-giant-genitalia-spark-outrage-at-the-brooklyn-museum/
5. Mayo Clinic Staff. "Pet Therapy: Animals as Healers." Mayo Clinic. 2018. https://www.mayoclinic.org/healthy-lifestyle/consumer-health/in-depth/pet-therapy/art-20046342
6. Peta. "The Egg Industry." Peta. 2020. https://www.peta.org/issues/animals-used-for-food/factory-farming/chickens/egg-industry/
7. Mark D. Griffith, PhD. Author. "The Psychology of Animal Torture." Psychology Today, 2016. https://www.psychologytoday.com/us/blog/in-excess/201611/the-psychology-animal-torture
8. Farm Sanctuary vs. USDA. "Protecting Pigs from Cruel High-Speed Slaughter." Animal Legal Defense Fund, 2020. https://aldf.org/case/protecting-pigs-from-cruel-high-speed-slaughter/
9. Tamika Mallory. Speaker. 2020. https://www.youtube.com/watch?v=kUvGeEQidT0
10. Sentient Media. "Effects of Deforestation." 2010. https://sentientmedia.org/how-does-agriculture-cause-deforestation/#:~:text=Around%206.7%20million%20acres%20of,other%20commodity%20in%20the%20region.

11. Erica Hellerstein and Ken Fine. Authors. "A Million Tons of Feces and an Unbearable Stench: Life Near Industrial Pig Farms." The Guardian, 2017. https://www.theguardian.com/us-news/2017/sep/20/north-carolina-hog-industry-pig-farms
12. Animals for Australia. "Why the Artificial Insemination of Turkeys is a Feminist Issue." Animals for Australia, 2011. https://www.animalsaustralia.org/media/opinion.php?op=151
13. Food Empowerment Project. "Slaughterhouse Workers." Food Empowerment Project, 2020. https://foodispower.org/human-labor-slavery/slaughterhouse-workers/

Drop 11:
1. Emily Hill. Author. "What is Being in the Zone?" Huffpost.com, 2017. https://www.huffpost.com/entry/what-it-really-means-to-b_b_10300610

Nectar Bowl

(A Place to Collect Your Thoughts)

Made in the USA
Monee, IL
28 October 2021